D1033962

Letters from Tommy J.

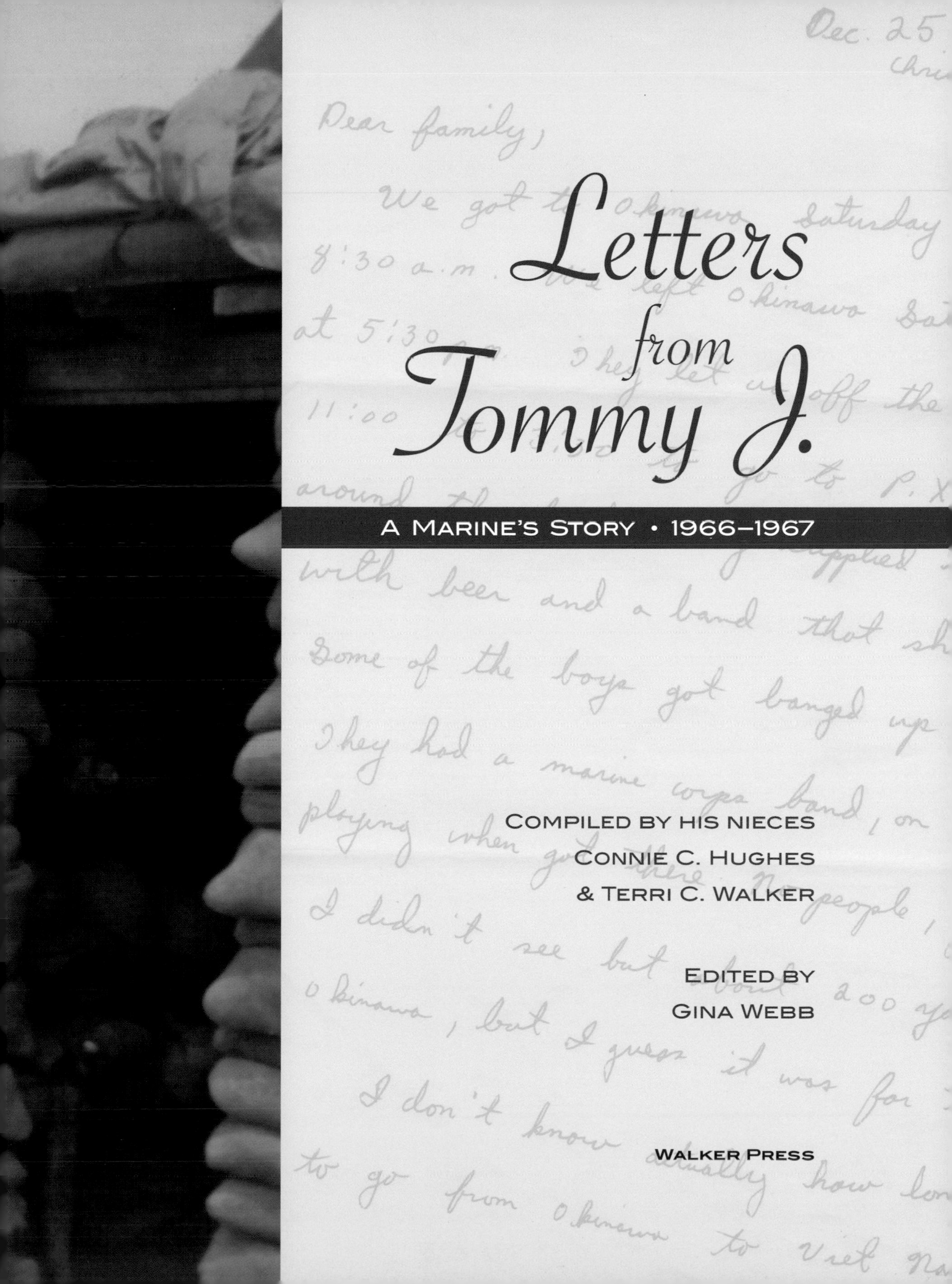

Letters from Tommy J.

A Marine's Story • 1966–1967

Compiled by his nieces
Connie C. Hughes
& Terri C. Walker

Edited by
Gina Webb

Walker Press

Copyright © 2008 Terri C. Walker
Published by Walker Press
4279 Roswell Road, #102-246
Atlanta, GA 30342
Telephone: 404-788-5411
Facsimile: 404-288-0816
www.terricwalkerconsulting.com
E-Mail: TCWlkr@aol.com

All rights reserved. No part of this publication may be reproduced in any form or by any electronic or mechanical means, including information storage and retrieval systems, without permission in writing from the publisher, except by reviewer who may quote brief passages in a review.

While every attempt has been made to provide accurate information, the author and publisher cannot be held accountable for any errors or omissions.

Designed and produced by Shock Design & Associates, Inc.
shockdesign@mindspring.com
www.shockdesign.com

Manufactured in Korea

ISBN number: 978-0-9720522-9-0
LC number: 2007936319

Picture credits
Pages viii–ix: Department of Defense
Page v: U.S. Marine Corps
Pages 24, 26 and 27: Library of Congress
All other images belong to the Holtzclaw, Walker and Hughes family archives

This book was inspired by letters written by Thomas James Holtzclaw III, while he was in Vietnam between December 15, 1966 and April 21, 1967.

"With confidence in our armed forces, with the abounding determination of our people, we will gain the inevitable triumph... so help us God."

— President Franklin D. Roosevelt

This is dedicated to all those who have served and are serving in the Armed Forces of the United States of America, as well as for some who are near and dear to our hearts:

Joe Labarbera, U.S. Army

James Dustin Sidwell, Lance Corporal, Marine Corp

Clinton Matthew Sidwell, Specialist, National Guard

Also in memory of Tony Brown, Master Sergeant
National Guard (Madison, Georgia)

USA's Forgotten Heroes

Thank you to those who have the "courage, sacrifice, and devotion to duty and country" to answer their country's call.

Contents

Preface

The Vietnam War was the longest war in our nation's history. It had its beginnings when North Vietnam announced its "armed struggle" with South Vietnam in 1959. In July of that year, the first American casualties occurred when two U.S. military advisors were killed by Viet Cong at Bien Hoa. The final incident of the war took place in May 1975, when Khmer Rouge forces seized the American ship SS *Mayagüez* in recognized international sea lanes claimed as territorial waters by Cambodia and removed its crew for questioning. The subsequent battle resulted in the deaths of 41 U.S. servicemen. The last American soldiers in Vietnam—ten Marines—left Saigon on April 30, 1975.

For the Vietnamese, the war was even longer. It began a century before, when the French invaded the country in the 19th century, plundered its natural resources and renamed their possession Indochina. During World War II, Vietnam threw off the yoke of French colonialism, fought free of the occupying Japanese in 1940, and again beat the French in 1954 at Dien Bien Phu. Divided into North and South by the Geneva Convention, Vietnam waited in vain for free elections promised in the treaty to reunify the country. Instead, President Diem declined to hold elections, fearing a communist victory, and U.S. President Dwight D. Eisenhower began sending military advisors into Vietnam to help fight the spread of communism. Ho Chi Minh, the leader of the North Vietnamese forces, marshaled his forces to overthrow the South Vietnamese government, and the resulting conflict lasted sixteen years and was handed off from one U.S. president to another.

After John F. Kennedy's assassination in 1963, Lyndon B. Johnson inherited the war, which had become unpopular in the U.S. due to the fact that many people believed that America was interfering with Vietnam's struggle for unification. Johnson did not want to be perceived as "soft" on the spread of communism, but was reluctant to commit more troops; in the spring of 1964, however, fewer than 150

American soldiers had died in Vietnam. Only after a US destroyer was fired upon in August by North Vietnamese torpedo boats in the Gulf of Tonkin, did Congress authorize Johnson to escalate the war using air strikes and committing ground forces.

In March of 1965, Johnson launched Operation Rolling Thunder, a series of bombing raids that would take place on a regular basis, and sent the first "official" U.S. combat troops to South Vietnam, the 3,500-man 9th Marine Expeditionary Brigade, which landed at the beaches northwest of Da Nang. It was assumed that sufficient American forces would put a swift end to the North Vietnam resistance. The build-up was rapid enough that by July, America had 125,000 troops stationed in Vietnam; by December, troop levels had reached 385,300. But the enemy was growing in number as well. Isolated bombing proved inadequate to reach the well-concealed Viet Cong, guerrilla fighters who now were being joined by well-trained, well-equipped North Vietnamese soldiers. As the NVA/VC ranks swelled, ground forces were sorely needed to carry out search and destroy missions in strategic areas considered to be VC strongholds and to defeat enemy forces that had massed close to and were assaulting U.S. air force bases.

One of these was Da Nang, an air base about 475 miles south of Hanoi and 600 miles north of Saigon, where approximately 6,000 enemy forces were known to be gathered in the vicinity in late 1966. Into this mounting conflict, poured hundreds of U.S. soldiers, each one eager for battle and the opportunity to defend his country. One of them was an 18-year-old honor student from Atlanta, Georgia, nicknamed Tommy J.

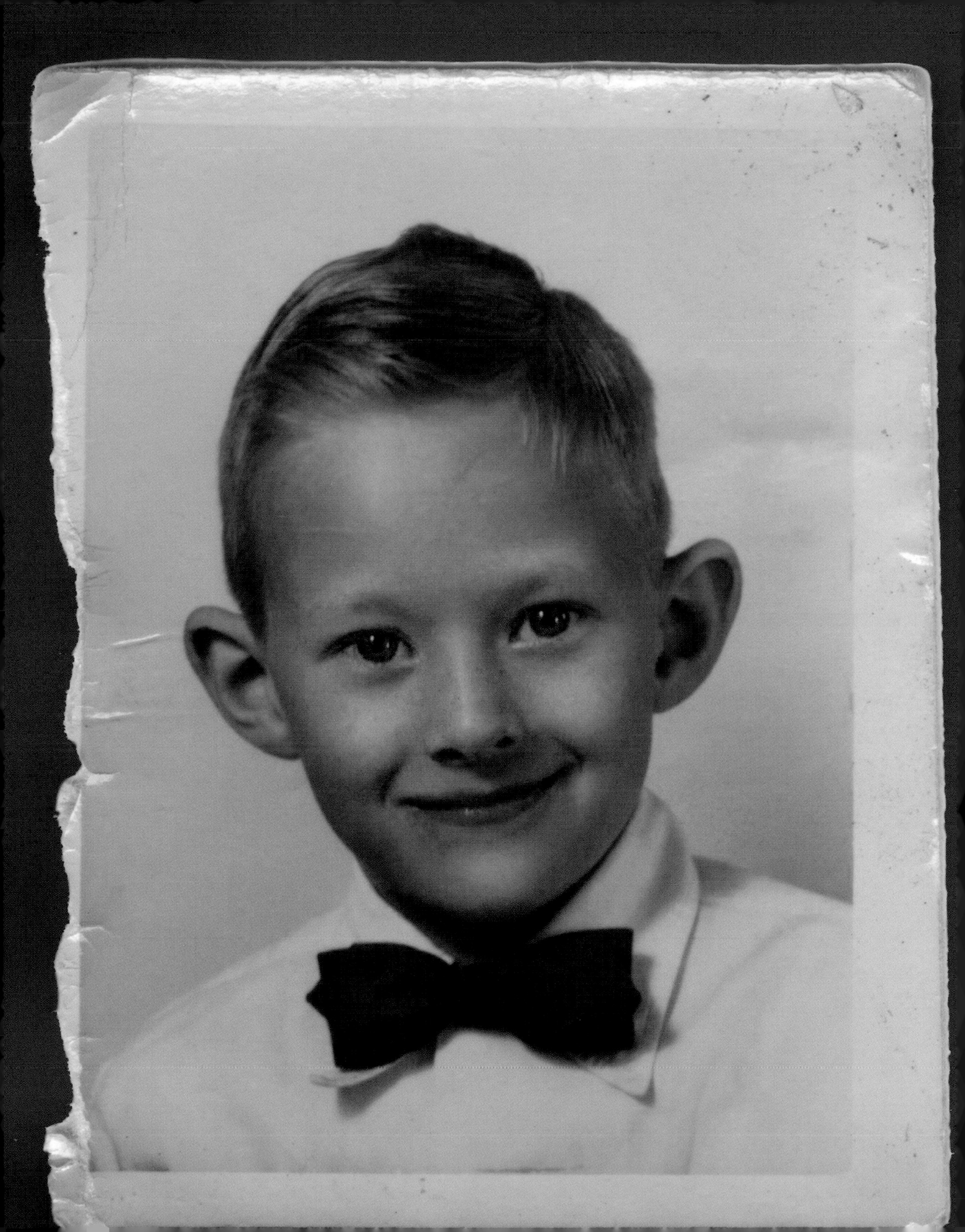

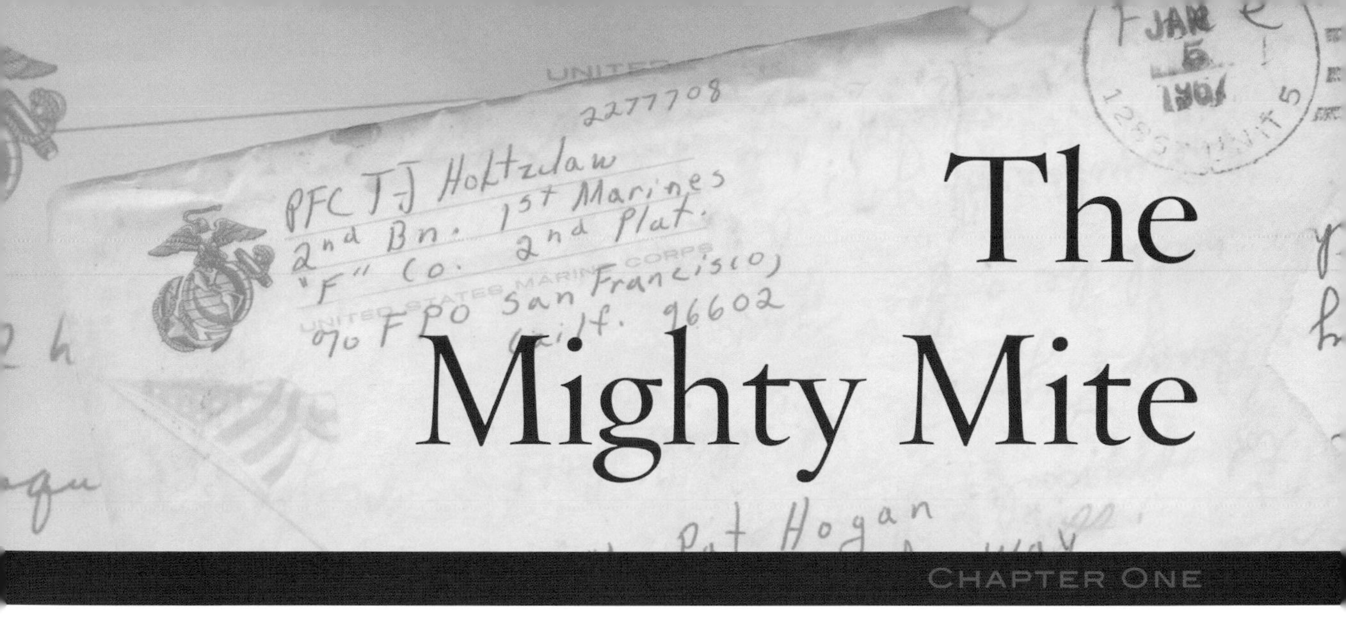

The Mighty Mite

CHAPTER ONE

"The mill villages were a society unto themselves—mill house, mill store, mill money, mill electricity, etc. When [Tommy] and I were kids, Atlanta had multiple mill villages: 'Exposition' (us), 'Fulton Bag' a/k/a 'Cabbage Town,' 'Whittier Mills,' and 'Avondale' are some that I remember. All basically the same, they even included a sports league that competed with one another."

— STEVE HOGAN

Thomas James Holtzclaw III was born April 24, 1948, at the Saint Francis Hospital in Greenville, South Carolina. His mother, Leila Mae Davis Holtzclaw, named Tommy after her brother, Thomas Davis, who was killed at age 19 in October 1944 in Paris, France, when stationed with the infantry during World War II. His father, Thomas James Holtzclaw, was a veteran of World War II employed by the Jackson cotton mill in Iva, a small town southeast of Greenville. With all the Thomases in the family—everyone called Mr. Holtzclaw "T.J."—the newest addition ended up with his own nickname: "Tommy J.", the name his family and most of his friends called him.

ABOVE: Thomas Davis, Tommy J.'s uncle, who was killed in WWII in 1944. OPPOSITE AND ABOVE LEFT: Tommy J.

Tommy was the middle child. His older sister, Jean, had been born in 1940 and his younger brother, Johnny, would come along in 1951. The family moved from South Carolina in 1960, when T.J. took a job as supervisor at the Exposition cotton mill in Atlanta. Life near the mill was a world in itself, a tightly knit community for which the mill owners provided health care, daycare and housing, and Tommy, starting seventh grade, quickly made friends at school.

Tommy J.'s parents, T.J. and Leila Holtzclaw

Siblings left to right: Johnny, Jean and Tommy J.

Blair Village School, Miss Drake's sixth & seventh grade 1959-60. Tommy J. is in the top row, second from the left

Tommy's best friend was Patrick Hogan, whose family, also members of the Exposition Mills neighborhood in NW Atlanta, lived about five miles from the Holtzclaws, who had moved to a house on Sumter Street in 1964. From the time they met in ninth grade, the two were inseparable. "We hit it off from the start," Pat remembered. "I mean from the very start. We were fast friends from the git go!" Mrs. Hogan recalled the boys spending all their time at each other's houses, and they remained close throughout high school, where both took part in student affairs and sports, even walking down the aisle together at graduation. Typical teenagers, they both loved "small cars, big dances, football, the gang," as Tommy would put it later in a letter. Patrick, thinking back on their friendship, said he could tell Tommy "anything. I mean anything."

While he was still only 15, but eager to take on responsibilities, Tommy (with his father's help) finagled a driver's license that listed his age as 16. He and another friend, Jimmy Portwood, delivered produce around Atlanta in a side-panel pickup. The store the two worked for was called the "Fruit Stand" by young people at the time. It had at least three locations, one on Hemphill Avenue, one downtown and one on Ponce de Leon. The two boys delivered vegetables and fruits in boxes to the other stores. Jimmy recalled leaving "about six to eight boxes of tomatoes in the streets of downtown Atlanta taking the turns a little too fast. We never stopped to retrieve the goods as most were crushed by the cars behind us."

Tommy J. in his football uniform

Tommy attended O'Keefe High School in Atlanta, Georgia, where he had letters in football, soccer, basketball, track and wrestling. He was also a solid A and B student who never missed a practice or an assignment in football and soccer. He was a member of the Honor Club, Student Government, Beta Club and Junior Civitan Club. He belonged to the Military Officer's Club, the Science Club and the French Club. He also served as homeroom president, was a senior superlative, and was in the top 10% of his class. He was treasurer of the student government, the Coed HiY Club and the Dance Club.

Tommy J.'s face shows up again and again in the 1966 Ke-O-Ke (O'Keefe's yearbook). Solemn, composed and wearing a suit in most of the pictures, Tommy was in a hurry to grow up.

Athletics at O'Keefe—whose school fight song was the same as Notre Dame's—provided another arena for close friendships to develop. Pat Hogan's two older brothers—Steve and Mike—played football, and Pat and Tommy became enthusiastic and devoted athletes. Along with taking part in track and wrestling, Tommy was a reserve halfback in football and first-string wingback two years in soccer. His coach, Dan Kennerly, described him as "a 125-pounder with the heart of a 250-pounder," and referred to Tommy as a "mighty mite" of O'Keefe's "Fighting Irish" football and soccer teams. Close friends remember that though he was too slight of build to play that often, Tommy was "a loyal bench sitter."

Kaye Bowman

He was the kind of kid who had, as his friend Jimmy Portwood says, "many friends [and dates] in school." Kaye Bowman, Tommy's high school girlfriend, was a sophomore when he met her in 1965. They dated throughout his senior year and as time went on, Tommy hoped that their relationship would develop into something permanent. Tommy was loyal and devoted to his family and friends. He belonged to the Marantha Baptist Church in Atlanta, Georgia, and would later ask that part of his military pay go toward his tithes. He was an avid boy scout who would later write his friend Pat that the Marines were "a little harder than Boy Scout Camp."

T.J. Holtzclaw had fought in World War II, where he was stationed in the Pacific. Eager for battle, he'd ignored symptoms of a ruptured appendix, went ashore to fight anyway, and endured an emergency appendectomy in the field. He had even lied about his age (26) in order to enlist. Despite his enthusiasm and bravery, when he was honorably discharged in 1946, T.J. came out questioning the war in general, with a life-long hatred of the Japanese for their brutal treatment of American P.O.W.s. All three of Leila's brothers had joined the service and gone to war, but only one had come back. Neither she nor T.J. wanted their sons to experience the harsh realities of war.

Tommy, though, had different ideas. In high school, he successfully completed two years of instruction in the Junior Division, Reserve Officers Training Corps (ROTC) and became eligible in 1965 to enlist in the Army Reserve in the grade of Private (E2). Before graduating

Kaye Bowman and Tommy at O'Keefe Senior Prom

from O'Keefe in June 1966, and against his parents' wishes and advice, Tommy enlisted in the United States Marine Corps. It was one secret that he did not share with Pat Hogan, or anyone else, until all that was left was for his parents to sign off on his enlistment papers. He was still 17 years old.

Mike Hogan, a year ahead of Tommy, joined the Marines the same

". . . Intelligence is a mainspring of a delightful personality. Deliberate and reserved, he assumes responsibility and takes initiative."

—Ke-O-Ke 1966

year. His parents, Skip and Jean, who had married during WW II, had never envisioned another war, especially one that would involve their own children. But Patrick was drafted into the Army in 1969; Steve Hogan served from 1970-71. Said Steve later of his own, his brothers' and Tommy J.'s zeal to serve: "We are sons of the 'Greatest Generation,' who were reared that we all owe our country." In Tommy's case, he made his commitment loud and clear by signing up for a three-year term.

His next step was Camp LeJeune in North Carolina, where he

United States Marine Corps

Certificate of Acceptance

This is to certify that Thomas James Holtzclaw III has successfully passed the required mental, moral and physical examinations and has been accepted for enlistment in the United States Marine Corps.

The defense of our country and our freedoms is the duty and privilege of every citizen. The Marine Corps has a proud tradition of outstanding service to our country in peace and war. Voluntary enlistment in this elite military organization is a clear demonstration of those American qualities of patriotism and loyalty to God and country.

Presented this 15th day of March, 1966.

By the Officer In Charge
Marine Corps Recruiting Station

NAVMC 6648 (Rev.)

would complete the course prescribed by the Commandant of the Marine Corp, and was assigned Military Occupational Specialty 0311 - Marine rifleman, possibly the most common and most hazardous military occupation the Marines had to offer. Since the war in Vietnam was primarily a ground war, the U.S. Marine Corps would play an important role, furnishing most of the American combat units in the Military Corps area (I Corps) that comprised northeast South Vietnam. Tommy's training readied him for exactly the kind of approach that General Westmoreland had determined was needed to combat the North Vietnamese Army and the Viet Cong: anticipating guerrilla warfare through search and destroy missions, combat patrols and ambushes rather than front-line battles.

Tommy believed wholeheartedly in the quote on his certificate of acceptance: "*The defense of our country and our freedoms is the duty and privilege of every citizen. The Marine Corps has a proud tradition of outstanding service to our country in peace and war. Voluntary enlistment in this elite military organization is a clear demonstration of those American qualities of patriotism and loyalty to God and country.*"

Yet in a letter to Patrick Hogan from LeJeune only a few months after his enlistment, Tommy was already questioning his rash decision. Only to Pat, though, would he ever admit these second thoughts.

1020
FIRST RECRUIT BATTALION
SSGT. F. BAKER
PLATOON 1020
SSGT. S.J. DRAPER
GRADUATED 7 - SEPT. - 1966

Tommy J. is in the 3rd row down from the top, 7th from the left

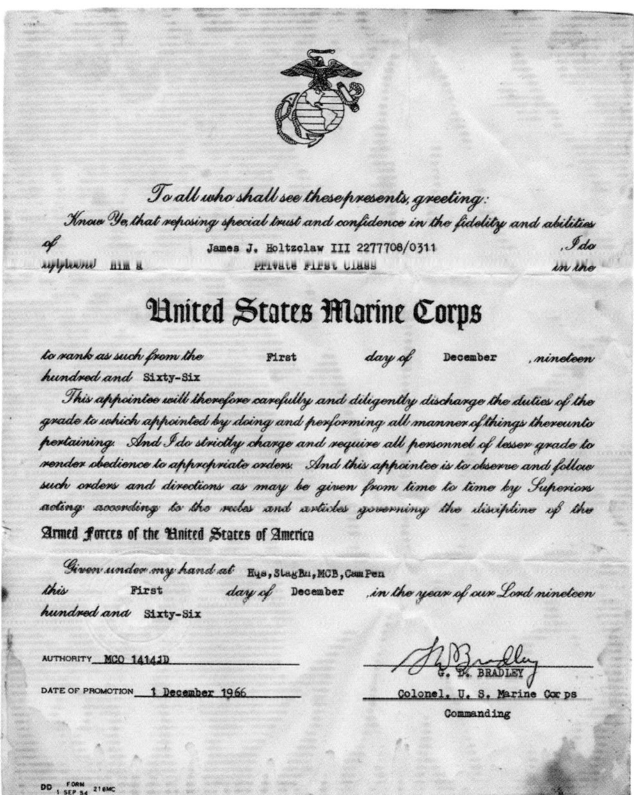

To all who shall see these presents, greeting:

Know Ye, that reposing special trust and confidence in the fidelity and abilities of James J. Holtzclaw III 2277708/0311 *, I do appoint* him a Private First Class *in the*

United States Marine Corps

to rank as such from the First *day of* December *, nineteen hundred and* Sixty-Six

This appointee will therefore carefully and diligently discharge the duties of the grade to which appointed by doing and performing all manner of things thereunto pertaining. And I do strictly charge and require all personnel of lesser grade to render obedience to appropriate orders. And this appointee is to observe and follow such orders and directions as may be given from time to time by Superiors acting according to the rules and articles governing the discipline of the Armed Forces of the United States of America

Given under my hand at Hqs, StagBn, MCB, CamPen *this* First *day of* December *, in the year of our Lord nineteen hundred and* Sixty-Six

AUTHORITY MCO 1414.1D

DATE OF PROMOTION 1 December 1966

G. D. BRADLEY
Colonel, U. S. Marine Corps
Commanding

DD FORM 1 SEP 54 216MC

The U.S. Marine Corp misnamed Tommy J. on his certificate of acceptance.

Sunday, Sept. 18, 1966

Dear Pat,
Got your letter, glad to hear your cheerful pen. You are really a pal, and have always been. Ever since the 8th grade. Remember? Small cars, big dances, football, the gang. Boy I sure wish we could go back to it. Now it is a little more serious. We both have to grow up and start making plans. Mine are made for 3 years. You can really make something for yourself. Just get your schooling down. You'll be real prosperous.

I honestly wished I hadn't come in, but it is too late. Don't tell Mom and Daddy I said that, they'll get depressed.

I'll be home around Oct. 15th, so fun will commence then.

This camp is real hard. Only time I get off is Sunday mornings. Don't even have time to write at night. It is a little harder than Boy Scout Camp was.

I heard O'Keefe pulled it through against Murphy. Maybe they will snap out of it now.

Well I will write again soon.

Your pal,

Tommy

Wednesday, Oct. 12, 1966

Hi Pal,
I hope you are well and happy. I am both right now. I just found out I get 30 days leave before going to California for staging. That is a pretty long time. I get to leave for home Oct. 19th and will be home by that night. One week from today, I'll be there. But I'll be tied up that night for sure, but maybe I will see you Thursday if you don't have many classes.

We still have 4 days of hard training left. 2 days we will be out all day and night fighting a simulated war. Living in foxholes and things and it sure gets cold at night. I got to think of something to stay warm a little.

I can't wait till I get home, to raise that cain we are going to do. Atlanta had better watch out, because I got to do enough to last me a year or more.

I called home and heard about Homecoming. Good enough. I have to close now. See you Thursday, I hope.

Tommy J.

On December 1, 1966, Tommy J. was appointed Private First Class by the 1st Infantry Training Regiment at Camp Pendleton, California, and became a member of the 1st Marines, the oldest and most decorated division-sized unit in the United States Marine Corps. On December 9, 1966, he boarded a Navy transporter ship called the U.S. General H.J. Gaffey. It left San Diego, California, en route to Okinawa, from where it would then head to Vietnam.

Note: No letters from Tommy's days in basic training are available. The letters home to his family begin with those he wrote onboard ship en route to Southeast Asia.

Leaving Home

CHAPTER TWO

Three million US soldiers served in Vietnam between 1965 and 1973. The average age of the soldier fighting in Vietnam was 19—seven years younger than soldiers had been in World War II, and far more vulnerable to the psychological strains, whether it was climate, the inability to distinguish civilians from combatants, or the constant threat of death. The U.S. Army drafted soldiers at the age of eighteen and, to protect them from the stress of war, limited their terms to just over a year. Marines, rarely draftees, signed up for anything from 13 months to a three-year term.

"We didn't see the big picture from our vantage point; just the day to day, hour-to-hour at the bottom rung of the ladder. The grunts [infantry] describe it as the "100 yard War" because that's all you could see (sometimes less) and have some control over. The control part was always debatable."

— STEVE HOGAN

Even though Viet Nam was a household word by 1966, the country was still an exotic and unknown destination for a raw recruit and someone as young as Tommy. Like all Americans, he watched the nightly news to see the latest battles, which featured sound effects and body counts, the exhausted faces of soldiers and the occasional Viet Cong prisoners, looking bedraggled and barely clothed. Basic training had taught Tommy what he knew about Vietnam's history or what he would encounter there—guerrilla warfare, jungle survival, what to do if captured by the enemy. But what Tommy and the rest of his countrymen didn't learn about was the individual soldier, whose day-to-day existence was unimaginable: conducted far from civilization or even the simplest comforts. This soldier's invisible enemy attacked on their own terms, without provocation, warning or any regard for traditional military rules of battle.

Other than his trip to North Carolina for basic training, Tommy J. had never traveled far from his hometown, never been on a ship, and never been away from his family for longer than the weeks he spent at boy-scout camp. Beginning with the letters from onboard ship, Tommy wrote home almost every day.

OPPOSITE: The U.S. General H. J. Gaffey, docked in San Diego, California prior to taking Tommy J. and his fellow marines to Okinawa, Japan en route to Vietnam.

Thursday, Dec. 15

Dear Folks,
I am into my sixth day at sea and it seems like 600. I can't mail any letters till I get to Okinawa, so I am writing a little bit all along the way. This is the first time I have felt like writing. I have been seasick since we started. It was the worse sickness I ever had. I finally went to sick-bay and got a shot and some pills. I feel a little better now.

This is the 1st ship I have ever been on, and I hope the last. Let daddy tell you all the bad things about a troop carrier and you will know what kind of ship I am on. It is terrible! If it gets much more cramped up in here, I will probably jump over the side of the ship. I never want to be a prisoner.*

It takes all day to eat 3 meals, if you feel like eating, plus we have working parties on the ship.

I think we are suppose to hit Okinawa in about 14 days from when we started. We will probably only be there a short while. Not even enough time to get off the ship.

Tonight we cross the International Date Line which means we will skip a day. This will put us a day ahead of Atlanta.

I hope you are all well and getting ready to have a big, happy Christmas. I will be thinking of you. I am going to eat the fruit cakes Xmas day and let some of the boys have some. I still have the 2 presents Jean and J.C. gave me to open. I hope everyone likes the things I bought for you and know how much I really love you all.

Will write some more later.

Tommy J.

P.S. The ship's name is U.S. Gen. Gaffey. Also, in your next letter, tell me the last name of my cousin in the Marines, Butch______?
I wouldn't even know him if I ever saw him.

---

* The U.S.S. Gaffey held a total of 2000 men, including enlisted and officers. It was 600 feet long and roughly 75 feet wide.

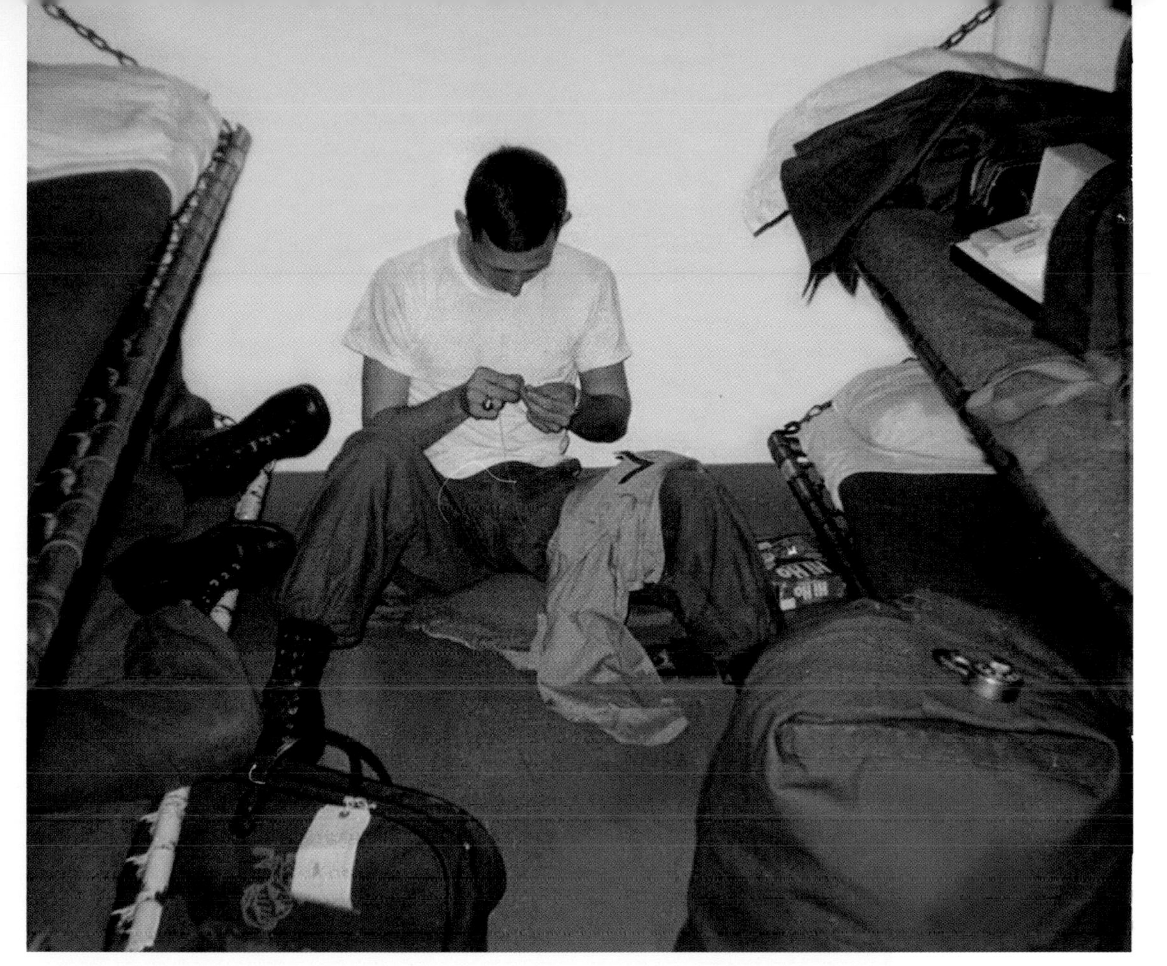

Tommy J. sewing stripes on his uniform in his cabin on the U.S.S. Gaffey

Saturday, Dec. 17

Dear folks,
We shipped that day during the night. Funny how it works. It has got me all messed up.

I have been watching different movies at night now. They are some relaxation. Other times I play cards or some game. At least it keeps my mind off being sick.

I feel somewhat better now, and I am starting to eat again. I don't need to lose weight, that is for sure.

While I am thinking about it, I meant to tell you to take $10 out of the $60 check that starts coming at the end of Jan. and put it in the church for me. That will take care of my tithes.

Well there is not much to write about on the ship, so I will close for today. I love you all.

Tommy J.

Sunday, Dec. 18

Dear family,
I hope you are all well today. It has been quite hot on the ship today, and that is quite different. I am going to have a little trouble getting use to being hot again.

Today I finally saw something besides water and ship; a sea gull flew by. We are suppose to be close to a bunch of small islands. There are a lot of them on the map.

It is kind of hard to believe that I am overseas. I always remember when the old veterans talked about it, but now I get my own stories to tell. I hope I can apply what I have been taught and not mess up at anytime.

I will close for today. I love you all. Be good.

Tommy J.

Tuesday, Dec. 20

Dear family,
It seems like I'll never see land again. This is the only time the Marine Corps life has been so boring. They usually keep you occupied pretty well; but this sailing is so monotonous. The only thing I am learning is how to play a lot of different card games. I do find out a lot about other boys' cities and girls and experiences, because most of them love to talk about it.

I have been dying my white stuff green. You want everything to look like vegetation, because what good is it to shoot at a bush or tree. Ha Ha. I guess I will get pretty tired of green.

This time here when I can't get my mail is very bad. I hope I never have to go this long without it again. Time goes so slow and you feel stranded on a nowhere place and forgotten. I guess you see I feel pretty homesick today. I'll get better when something starts to happen.

Well the word was passed, we wouldn't have time for liberty in Okinawa. That is the way it goes.

I'll close for now.

Tommy J.

P.S. It is getting awful hot. We even started sunbathing.

Dec. 21, Wednesday

Dear family,
We just got through with a inspection of our living quarters. They have one every morning and they really expect a clean place. You should see how clean a place like this has to be. But Naval Officers do the inspecting and the Navy always was kinda stupid in certain ways, weren't they daddy? He He He.

I guess I will tell you about the incident that happened to me yesterday. I was in the game room when a fight broke out between a white guy and two negroes. I naturally being good-natured tried to break it up and when the MP's got there I couldn't convince them that was all I was doing so I was put into the brig for 2 days of "cooling off time." Around 7:30 last night I was let out because the white guy happened to be a Sgt. and he didn't have on his shirt so the colored boys didn't know it and they are in deep water. He thanked me and told me to go back to my living quarters. Boy was I glad. The brig is no place for me. I guess from now on, I'll just be a innocent looker.

Tommy J.'s father, T.J., in uniform

I can't get my friends to stop the kidding me, but it will pass over I guess.

*I hope everyone is well. How is the lot shaping up?**

I will close for today. I love you all.

Tommy J.

* The lot Tommy refers to was one his parents had bought and planned to build a cabin on. Plans for the cabin became a big factor in his own dreams of the future, and he often referred to his desire to be there, so he could help with the building.

Thursday, Dec. 22

Dear family,
Today is a overcast day, but it is warm. If all goes right, we should get to Okinawa Saturday and now the rumor is we will get a day of liberty. All I can say is just wait and find out. But it would do me most good if we did have a little time off.

Last night I played Bingo. They had about 10 jackpots, but I didn't win any. I was awful close. We also had a talent show, made up from the troops. They did singing, clowning, and played some instruments. It was real good.

They have put a Christmas tree up in the game room.

It really makes you feel a little lonesome. I don't know what will take place Christmas. We will probably have singing sessions.
I'll write more later.

Tommy J.

Friday, Dec. 23

Dear Daddy, Mother and Johnny,
This is the eve before the eve of Christmas eve. Still doesn't seem like Christmas. The setting's just not right.

Tomorrow we will dock at Okinawa for refueling. I still haven't heard any word on liberty. I guess this will be my last letter of the voyage so I can mail them tomorrow. I'll write again later to let you know what happens from there.

We went back another hour last night to Okinawa Standard Time. In all, I have gone back 10 hrs. since I left Atlanta, and skipped one day. So your guess is as good as mine on the different times.

How do you like my "Initiation Card" from the Golden Dragon Domain. The initiation was not too bad. The senior men aboard held the ceremony. All I had to do was bow to the king and do some singing. Some of the other boys really got it bad.

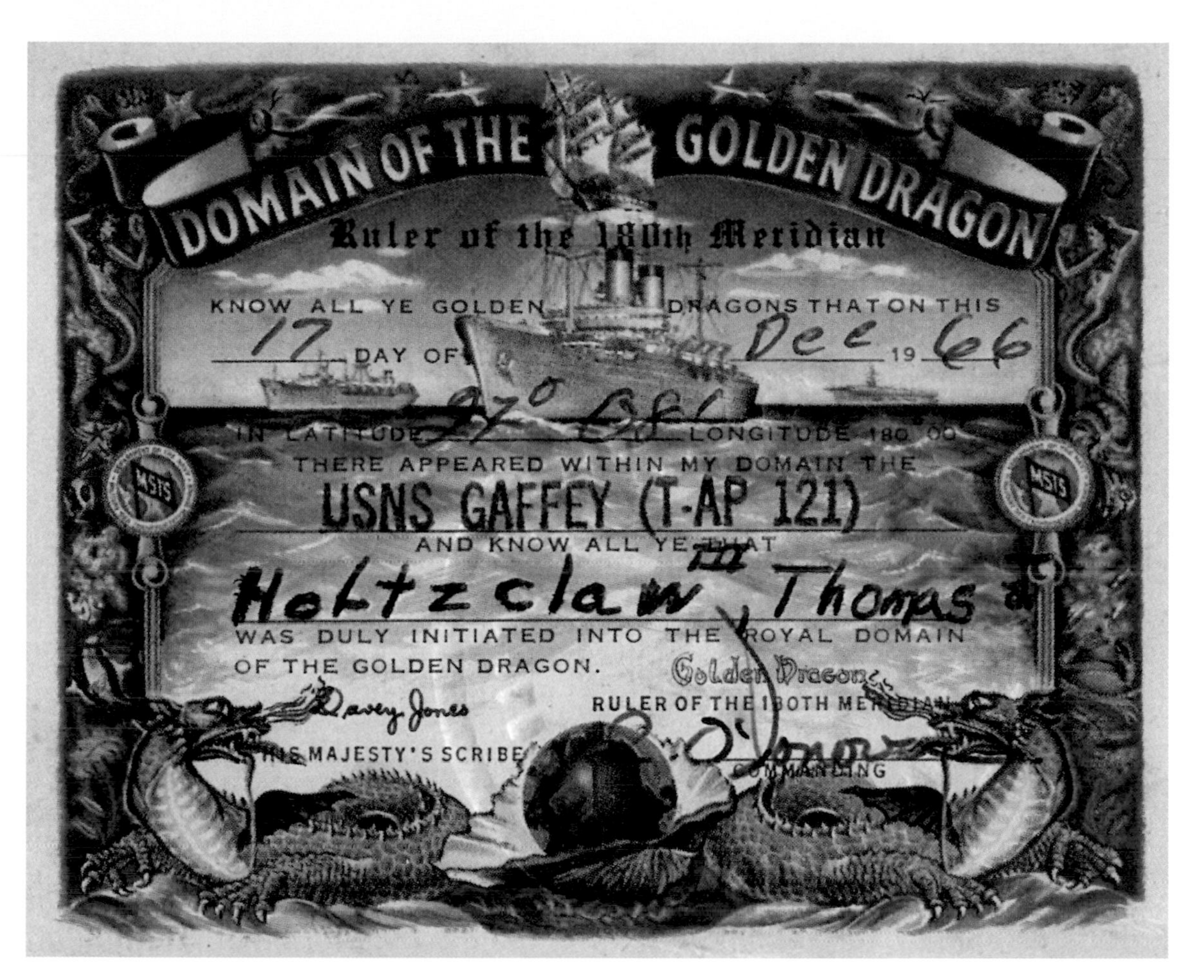

DOMAIN OF THE GOLDEN DRAGON

Ruler of the 180th Meridian

KNOW ALL YE GOLDEN DRAGONS THAT ON THIS 17 DAY OF Dec 19 66 IN LATITUDE 27° [illegible] LONGITUDE 180 00 THERE APPEARED WITHIN MY DOMAIN THE

USNS GAFFEY (T-AP 121)

AND KNOW ALL YE THAT

Holtzclaw III, Thomas

WAS DULY INITIATED INTO THE ROYAL DOMAIN OF THE GOLDEN DRAGON.

Davey Jones
HIS MAJESTY'S SCRIBE

Golden Dragon
RULER OF THE 180TH MERIDIAN

[illegible]
COMMANDING

The International Date Line at the 180 meridian. Traveling west across the Pacific, a time-honored tradition has it that anyone crossing by water is initiated into the "Domain of the Golden Dragon." At Tommy J.'s initiation, the ship's crew dressed up and led the blindfolded troops through a series of obstacles, including blood and fish parts. Upon completion of the course, the troops received a paddling.

I hope some letters are waiting in Okinawa tomorrow. I'll be thinking about you all Christmas. I hope you have a great time and have one for me too.

How is Johnny's soccer coming along? I know they had a rough time replacing last year's team. Ha. Good luck to them.

I will close so I can write later. Be good. I love you all.

Tommy J.

P.S. I was put on MP duty till we get to V. Nam. I have to guard the brig. They must want someone with experience. He He.

Dec. 25, Sunday Christmas

Dear family,
We got to Okinawa Saturday morning at 8:30 a.m. We left Okinawa Saturday evening at 5:30 p.m. They let us off the ship from 11:00 to 3:30 to go to the P.X. and just around the beach. They supplied the boys with beer and a band that short while. Some of the boys got banged up [drunk] pretty good. They had a Marine corps band, on the pier, playing when I got there. No people, just a band. I didn't see but about 200 yds. of Okinawa, but I guess it was for the better.

I don't know actually how long it takes to go from Okinawa to Viet Nam, but it is around 3 or 4 days.

Today is not much different from any other. I will go to church later, plus I have to go on guard duty this afternoon probably.

I guess I will write a little along the way to V. Nam and mail them when I get there.

I hope this day was very happy and fun to you all. I hope Jean and them got to come up O.K. Be good and have a good New Year's also. I love you all.

Tommy J.

P.S. I opened Jean and her families gifts. It was a cylinder flashlight and a utility knife. It was very nice. I'll eat the fruitcake today.*

Opposite: The view of Okinawa from the U.S.S. Gaffy

Monday, Dec. 26

Dear family,
It would be Christmas Day in Atlanta today. I hope it is going well for you.

I went to church and then we had a turkey dinner yesterday. We mostly just laid around. I opened the fruitcakes and passed them

---

* Tommy's sister, (Evelyn) Jean, had married James C. Campbell in July of 1962. Connie Lynn was born in April 1963, and Terri Ann in September 1964.

around. They were real good.

We will probably get to V. Nam tomorrow or Wednesday. They don't ever tell us anything. We got to get a shot today. A bad one in the rear end. It takes about 3 min. to give it. It is suppose to keep you from losing weight.

The closer I get to V. Nam the more nervous I get. I don't know what to expect about a place I can't believe I'm going to. I guess it won't take long to believe it though. I'll just keep on praying.

How did you like your presents? Did everything fit? I hope so. I have to thank Kaye on some of those selections and sizes. Sorry I didn't get Jean and them more.

We haven't gotten any letters yet. Sure has been a long time. I hope we get some real soon.

Well I will close for today. Be good. I love you all.

Tommy J.

Tuesday, Dec. 27

Dear family,
We are only a short ways from V. Nam now. We will get there this evening, but will stay on ship till Wednesday morning.

I found out that I am going to the 1st Division, 1st Regiment. As you know, the two regiments doing most of the fighting is the 1st and 5th. I am a scared person right now. Quite a few boys are that way. I know the location of the 1st, but I can't spell it so I will write that later. I hope you are still praying a lot, because I know now I need some help greater than what is on earth.

We will depart for our outfits Wednesday morning so when you get this letter, you can then say your son is well in V. Nam. Don't worry though, because I am proud in a way and I think I am growing up a lot. At least I know how to appreciate home and things. My ambition to

---

Note: Tommy was assigned to Company F, 2d Battalion, 1st Marines, 1st Marine Division. The 1st Division included the 1st, 5th, 7th, and 11th Marine Regiments.

make the most of myself is increasing a lot. I think a lot of the future now. I am hoping to put Kaye in my plans if she will wait. I know it is a long time, but I am hoping.

We got the shot yesterday. It wasn't as bad as I thought. Just a funny feeling.

I will mail this letter this evening so they can mail it tomorrow.

Don't be sad or worry, because I will do my best. Be good. I love you all.

Tommy J.

P.S. The 1st regiment is located north of Danang close to the separation line of North and South Viet Nam—the DMZ [demilitarized zone]. *They just told us. I don't know but about 2 boys who will go with me.*

NORTH VIETNAM
DEMARCATION LINE
QUANG TRI
Hue
I CTZ
LAOS
THUA THIEN
Da Nang
SOUTH CHINA SEA
THAILAND
QUANG NAM
QUANG TIN
QUANG NGAI
KONTUM
BINH DINH
SOUTH VIETNAM
PLEIKU
CAMBODIA
PHU BON
PHU YEN
Tonle Sap
DARLAC
II CTZ
KHANH HOA
QUANG DUC
TUYEN DUC
Da Lat
Cam Ranh
PHUOC LONG
BINH LONG
NINH THUAN
TAY NINH
III CTZ
LAM DONG
BINH DUONG
LONG KHANH
BINH THUAN
HAU NGHIA
BIEN HOA
BINH TUY
SAIGON
KIEN TUONG
CHAU DOC
KIEN PHONG
LONG AN
GIA DINH
PHUOC TUY
DINH TUONG
AN GIANG
SA DEC
GO CONG
Vung Tau
KIEN GIANG
VINH LONG
KIEN HOA
PHONG DINH
IV CTZ
VINH BINH
GULF OF THAILAND
CHUONG THIEN
BA XUYEN
BAC LIEU
AN XUYEN
SOUTH VIETNAM
1966–1967
Corps Tactical Zone Boundary
Administrative Boundary
Hue
Autonomous Municipality
0
150 Miles
0
150 Kilometers

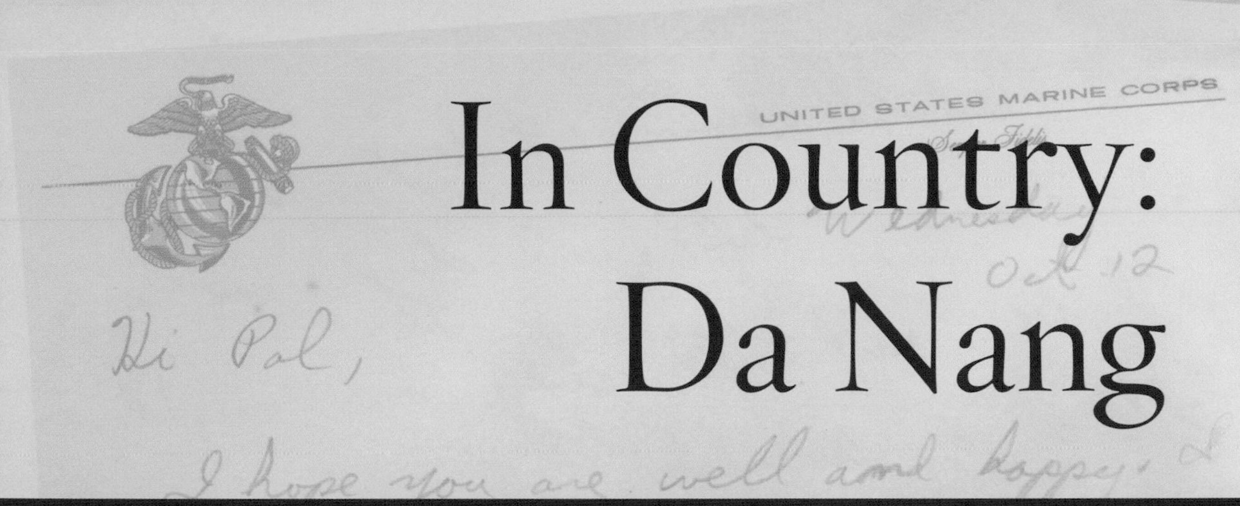

In Country: Da Nang

Chapter Three

The 1st Regiment of the Marines in 1966 were stationed in I Corps, the northeastern part of South Vietnam. Pronounced "eye" corps, the area comprised the five northern-most provinces and contained the port city of Da Nang, just south of the demilitarized zone (DMZ) at the 17th parallel. Fighting had been heavy in that zone throughout the year, and in October, U.S. Army combats units were introduced to provide reinforcement. The enemy had more than doubled in size, from 23 battalions in midsummer to 52 by the end of the year. During this era, refugees swarmed into Da Nang from the embattled countryside. Tommy J.'s first encounter with its population would be in the form of children, who begged for (and were given!) his dinner before he could eat it.

The next encounters he would have were not so innocent. The area surrounding Da Nang was heavily infested with Viet Cong, who were conducting a form of combat almost unheard of at that time. Prior to the war in Vietnam, American soldiers fought in an orderly manner, on battlefields, and in rows of troops. That was how it had been done in World War II and in every other war prior to that. But in Vietnam, everything changed.

Guerrilla warfare against American troops used three main tools: ambush, sabotage, and espionage. The jungle and mountain terrain in Vietnam facilitated this approach, making hiding and ambushes easier. Sympathetic villagers hid and protected the Viet Cong, allowing them to set mines and hide rice caches and weapons nearby which were the life blood of the guerrilla fighters. Battles were almost always sudden and unexpected. The North Vietnamese objective was to destabilize American troops through extensive, low-intensity confrontations to tie them up in unexpected battles for no real reason—a tactic that lowered morale, caused psychological terror, and gave the NVA the upper hand.

Finding the enemy was one of the biggest challenges to the American forces. The Viet Cong had created extremely complex and intricate tunnel systems over vast regions of South Vietnam, built over a period of 25 years, beginning in the 1940s when they fought the French and Japanese. The tunnels allowed the Viet Cong to control a large rural area, and formed an underground city with living area, kitchens, storage, weapon factories, hospitals, and command centers. They could be several stories deep and house up to 10,000 people.

For the North Vietnamese troops, these tunnels were fighting bases, capable of providing continuous support. The bases were well hidden from American spotter planes, and the remote swamps and forests provided ample cover from air and ground alike. Vents were installed in order to hear approaching helicopters. Smaller vents were used for air. There were hidden doors and punji traps. At deeper levels, there were chambers for arms factories and a well for a steady water supply. There were storage rooms for weapons and rice, and hospitals for guerrillas. Communication tunnels connected one base with another. The tunnels not only allowed guerrilla communication, but they allowed surprise attacks, even within the U.S. military bases.

"Bouncing Betty" mine

Weaponry changed. The Viet Cong arsenal—handmade but deadly—included booby traps, pits, rocket-propelled grenades, mortars, and recoilless rifles. Recovered American shells and bombs were turned into traps, mines, or another explosive devices. One of the most common, and hated, mines was nicknamed the "Bouncing Betty." It was triggered by the release of pressure on the mechanism. The soldier could stand on a Bouncing Betty, hear the arming mechanism operate and know perfectly well that if he moved his foot, the mine would jump in the air and blow up at chest height. Mortars were easily portable and easy to operate, their main appeal being their extensive flight time. A mortar team could set up a position out of the sight of the enemy, fire a number of rounds, and be moving away from the firing sight before the first rounds even hit their target.

The list of non-explosive booby traps was just as deadly, including punji stakes, bear traps, crossbow traps, spiked mud balls, double-spike caltrops, and scorpion-filled boxes. The punji stake was by far the most

Marines landing at Da Nang

common booby trap weapon. It was a shoot of bamboo or metal with needle-like tips that had been hardened by fire. These tips were often coated with excrement, poison or other contaminants to cause infection. Designed to "fix," or locate American troops, punji stakes caused a wound that, if not treated within 24 hours, often required amputation. When victims were medivaced out, the Viet Cong often shot down the helicopters.

When Tommy J. arrived at the Da Nang air force base, he was assigned to Fox Company, 2nd battalion. The second Battalion, 1st Marine Division had recently completed its participation in Operation Hastings during which many of its members had been wounded or killed, including the commanding officer. Captain Gene Deegan assumed command of Fox Company during late August 1966. Deegan was well-liked and respected, with a genuine concern for his men. In Fox Company, Tommy's job would be to conduct search and destroy missions, and run ambushes and combat patrols.

Tommy J.'s first view of Da Nang

Thursday, Dec. 28

Dear family,
I am here! We got off the ship this morning at Danang and were split up to our different organizations. They then trucked me to my Battalion area and I was assigned to a company and platoon. My platoon is out in the field right now on a mission. They won't be back till tomorrow. Only 6 boys are in the platoon with me from the whole draft and I don't know any of them.

Viet Nam was quite a shock. The people, the houses and stores and everything. I was trying to eat dinner, but all the kids kept begging for it, so I gave most of it away.

They only have tents for us to sleep in and there is only mud and rain right now. The monsoon season is still on. I was issued a rifle immediately when I got here and told I must carry it everywhere. To eat, sleep, and anywhere I go. We get our combat and jungle gear in the morning.

I don't know if I will ever get the mail you have mailed before this letter, or if it will take a long time if I do. Use the new address to get it here faster. Tell Kaye about it for me.

I am just north of Danang a little ways. It is not too nice right now. I see patrols going out tonight and they are all wet and muddy. Loaded down with ammunition and wearing all kinds of gear. I guess I'll be doing it soon.

I'll have to get all the U.S. money I have changed into some kind of V. Nam money. * *I don't know why.*

I guess I'll close and mail this. Don't worry.

I love you all.

Tommy J.

Sunday, Jan. 1, 67

Dear family,

I hope you have started off the New Year in good humor and spirits. I was standing guard on our line when the New Year came in. There were no horns or yells but it started a new year. It has rained every day I've been here. Just mud and rain. You can't keep dry or clean. It sure is a miserable feeling. The monsoon season should end next month, I hope. We will be leaving this area I am in now about tomorrow to move to a new location. We are going to an artillery location for 6 weeks. Then we come back here to the company area.

I will finish a 3 day indoctrination period today, in which you have to stay in the battalion area before going to the field. It is just a rule. This is a different war than I expected. You not only fight the V.C., you also fight the weather, snipers, and booby traps. Most of the company's wounds come from traps.

The platoon stands on a notice to be ready to go to an emergency anytime. They have 4 + 5 missions all the time. I guess I'll not get to write very often.

I have seen them bring in V.C. suspects, and dead V.C. It sure makes you that much more scared. I guess I'll overcome it though.

---

* Because the rate of exchange between the dollar and the Vietnamese piaster was so high in 1966, U.S. money had been withdrawn from circulation to prevent black-market activities. Tommy was paid with military certificates, or scrips, which were negotiable as money at all U.S. facilities.

Well, I must close now. Will write again later. I love you all.
Your son,

Tommy J.

P.S. We just got the word to pack up only essentials to move out tomorrow. Happy New Year

January 4, 1967

Dear Pat,
I hope this finds you well and in good spirits. I am in a new and exciting place. I guarantee you don't get bored.

All it has done is rain everyday. It will rain till the end of this month. Then the hot weather comes in.

We live in tents when we are not in the field. They don't stay in the tents too often. This is a bigger war than people think. Every time the platoon goes out, they get in a firefight with the V.C. I am just trying to get a little experience, but it sure is nerve-wracking. I get awful scared when I hear those bullets.

We are just north of Danang right now. The Regiment moves around a lot.

I sure miss home now. I am really learning how to appreciate home and those everyday things you don't think about. Maybe this will be a fast year.

Everywhere I go, I have to carry my weapon and ammunition. I eat, sleep, and go to the bathroom with it. Some friend. I hope it does its job.

How's your school coming along? I hope you and Patsy are getting along O.K.

Well I'll close for now and go hunting later on. Raise Hell for me!

Write if you get a chance. Your old pal,

Tommy J.
corresponding from the big rifle range.

Sunday nite, Jan. 8, 67

Dear family,
I have just been lifted up in spirits this evening, when I finally got a letter from you. It was written Dec. 31 and had the Kool-aid in it. Thanks alot. I haven't written lately because I have been becoming a veteran. We left Friday on a search and destroy mission — my first — and have just come back. Friday we captured 4 V.C. suspects and sent them to be interrogated. Friday afternoon we were helicoptered to an area where they had some V.C. trapped in a area. After landing, we were crossing about a 500 meter rice paddy when the V.C. opened up on us. My heart stopped, I know. I jumped into a rice paddy and was under water. Then I came to my senses and began to return fire. We assaulted their position and they fled. We killed 4 of them and that was my worst part. I am certain I killed one, because I aimed and shot at him when he ran. It is a awful feeling. I still can't get over it. They told a couple of us to put them in some raincoats and move them to a pick-up area.

I just couldn't do it. I couldn't even look at them. The Sgt. didn't make me do it. He said all new ones were like that. I am trying to look at it as if I had to kill him or be killed. This is a crazy war. I never thought war could be so nerve-wracking.

The rain still comes everyday. I can't keep dry clothes. I am going to need those socks you are sending. I have stopped wearing underwear; too much to dry out and it gives you a rash.

I haven't gotten the candy yet; I hope I get it though. I hope I get all the back mail. If you had anything important to tell me in those letters, tell them over.

We are on 10 min. standby right now. That means if they give the word, we have to be ready to move out in 10 min. I hope we don't go. I am so tired and feel still wet.

I will close and hit the rock; I mean cot. I love you all so much.

Your 1st son,

Tommy J.

Monday, Jan. 9, 67

Dear family,
I am writing this short letter just to ask you to send me a few articles I need and can't get here, because they don't have a P.X. where I am. I hope you don't mind and you can get some money out of the bank to pay for this and 2 packages of film I am sending home to have developed. They were taken at home, Camp Pendleton, Disneyland, and while on ship.

Send me the ones of you and Kaye back please.

I'll close now.

Articles

1. *Tooth brush*
2. *Lighter fluid*
3. *Small piece of steel wool*
4. *1" paint brush*

(cleaning gear for rifle I need)

5. *Pack of Razor Blades*
6. *About 6 Air Mail stamps for sending home film*
7. *Writing Paper (like this)*
8. *A candle for use for light. About 6" or 8" tall*

Above: Kaye and Tommy
Right: Disneyland

Jan. 10

I didn't get to mail this off yesterday. I got 5 letters and a box of fruitcake last night. Sure feel alot better. I finally got one from Kaye and Mom Davis also wrote. It was real nice of her — she said it was her first letter of the New Year. She also sent a dollar in it. I was surprised but glad. The Bowman's sent the cake.

We went out all last night and guarded a bridge that the V.C. had been firing at. They didn't come last night. I just got ate up by mosquitoes.

I guess we will have a patrol later on today. I'll close now. I love you all.

Tommy J.

P.S. Packages under 5 lbs. come by air mail. I hope you don't mind sending these things. They are just necessities. Don't worry if you can't send them.

Jan. 10, Tuesday

Dear Mom and Pop Davis,

I received your letter and was real glad to hear from you. It was one of the first letters I have gotten since I have been here.

The weather right now is rainy and cool. The monsoon season will not be over till Feb. Then the hot really begins. This rain makes it a big problem to keep clean and dry clothes. I'll be glad when it stops raining I think.

I spent Christmas on the ship and we got to Da Nang, South Viet Nam the 28th Dec. We had a turkey dinner and church services that day.

My company is now just north of Da Nang. We are working all around the Da Nang area. The Viet Cong are everywhere. We live in big tents and have to use cots to sleep on. But we can get pretty comfortable sometimes.

Mother and them send me everything I need so don't worry about me. Say hello to everyone and I'll write more later.

Love always,

Tommy J.

Mom and Pop Davis, Tommy J.'s grandparents

January 12, 67

Dear family,
I hope this finds you all well. I received your letters you had to remail today. I also got one from Kaye.

We have been on a 2 day operation called "Sparrell-Lark." [sic: "Sparrow-Lark"] *A search and destroy mission. Bombs were dropped and then we started sweeping through. Guess where we got hit again. You're right, in the rice paddy. We opened up firing like 3 or 4 divisions. We got to the other side and found 4 wounded V.C. women. The most of them had fled. We also captured one man. Women fight along with the men. It is hard to picture. After that action, we didn't see any more the rest of the time. Now I am back at the area and we have to guard the camp tonight. I guess I'll have a hard time catching up with my rest.*

I am glad you and the Bowmans got the packages I sent. I hope they were good.

Kaye told me about the present you gave her. It sounds real nice.

How is O'Keefe's soccer doing now? I guess they play as many games as we did last year.

Well I have to close and get ready to guard. I'll write more later.

By the way, I hate to ask again for something, but would you please send me a combination lock for a footlocker I made. Master lock will be fine. Thanks.

I love you all.

Tommy J.

Note: Forty-three large unit operations, involving a force of at least a battalion, were conducted in southern I Corps during the first six months of 1967, including Operations HASTINGS, UNION I and II. In addition, thousands of smaller operations supported the larger "sweeps," one of these being "Sparrow Lark." Between January and March 1967, the 1st Marine Division carried out over 36,000 company-size operations, patrols, and ambushes in the Da Nang Tactical Area.

Tommy J. sent these pictures of a captured Viet Cong home to his family.

Jan. 13, 1967

Dear family,
I didn't get to mail these as soon as I thought I would but maybe it is for the better. I got a big story to tell about what happened when we went out on the ambush this morning.

We had been out since about 4:30 a.m. and had not done anything. Then we started walking through some jungles around some villages which run along a river. It was about 7:30 a.m. and just as we came upon a hut, we spotted V.C. in it. They saw us, opened fire and took off. We returned fire and began to chase.

Just as we had almost lost them, we saw one of them just going down a hole in the ground. We had a hand grenade fixing to throw when one of our bullets got him and the grenade blew up. We started firing on the hole, throwing in grenades and smoke and everything. Then we thought all were dead. We only expected 2 in there. I guarded the hole as our squad leader started in. Just as he had got a little ways in the hole, a grenade came rolling out. We all jumped for our lives. The grenade went off and one of our boys got fragments in the cheeks and mouth. We fired more ammunition in the hole and started in again. We asked them to surrender and they said nothing. Finally, the squad leader pulled one of them out and he was dead. He had an American made weapon. We thought that was all, but when we went in further, we found two more and another American weapon with American gear and grenades. All, except one, were dead and blown all apart. I really got sick. We tried to keep him alive, but he finally died. We then radioed in our success and Headquarters was real happy. Just as we thought all was over, we started getting automatic fire from snipers across the river. They really had us in a fix. The bullets were hitting all around. The boy who was beside me got hit in the leg. He was from Georgia. I was shaking and in shock, because the bullets had me pinned down. I almost froze. Then some finally started firing back. I crawled up to the edge of the river and sprayed the whole area with bullets. We saw the V.C. running and we really laid it on. I don't think we killed him, because they couldn't find him. We had been fighting for about a hour or more. Finally, reinforcements got there because we only had 11 men out there. We called in a helecopter and got the wounded out. Both boys are going back to U.S. because it is their 3rd purple heart. One has only been here 4 months.

The communist V.C. had all kinds of documents, N. Viet Nam money and other stuff. They were in pitiful shape. I won't describe it.

I never thought I could be so scared. I don't think I can take this place. We only have 7 men in our squad now.

I am praying like I never prayed before.

I am now kind of ashamed to send this letter, because I know how you will start worrying. Please don't. It is my battle now. I have come back in and trying to rest. It is awful hard to believe war. I know why Daddy hates to see war pictures. I jump at the slightest noise now. I'll be unbelievable when I do come home.

I will close now. Just pray and please don't get upset. It will be awful if I knew I was harming you.

I love you all.

Your son,

Tommy J.

Que Son Valley

CHAPTER FOUR

Beginning in mid-January 1967, Foxtrot Company, under the control of Captain Deegan, was relocated to Nui Loc Son (Loc Son Mountain), an outpost halfway between Da Nang and Chu Lai overlooking the fertile Que Son Valley, located along the border of Quang Nam and Quang Tin provinces. The valley was viewed by communist forces as one of the keys to controlling South Vietnam's five northern provinces. It was rice-rich and considered an important source of supplies and food for both the North Vietnamese army and the Viet Cong, who required an estimated 34 tons of supplies per day to function.

F Company relieved the ARVN, or South Vietnamese, unit on Nui Loc Son and began operations under the direct control of Colonel Emil J. Radics' 1st Marines. Initially, F Company was confined to observation, close-in patrolling, and a number of light-action projects. Their presence on the hill was expected to improve relationships between the military and the Vietnamese living in the nearby villages. Night ambushes and daily and nightly patrols would make their presence known and break the enemy's hold on the valley below. However, the long-range plan was for the Marines to eventually force the existing 2nd NVA Division into open battle.

But with the buildup of NVA troops in the Valley, joining the already entrenched Viet Cong, these "hill battles" were to become some of the hardest fought and most intense of the war. In January, Tommy's letters describe the upcoming move and hint at what would soon be a much larger "operation."

Jan. 15, 67

Dear folks,
It is Sunday afternoon and I am just getting back from a squad patrol. We captured another V.C. and got fired upon again. The bullets were hitting all around us. We didn't return fire, but just double-timed out of there. We were in a bad location with just a few men. I just missed falling into a punji stick trap. My right foot went in but I jumped to the left soon enough. Boy was I scared.

There are 3 platoons in our company, and so far 1st and 3rd have had wounded casualties from mines in two days. About 15 in all. Our platoon has escaped so far. Say some prayers for everyone.

We will be leaving soon to go on a 7-day mission to an area which is suppose to be a look-out post. We only carry a little gear and live in bunkers and eat "C" rations. I know it will be exciting. They have quite a bit of action there. I may not get to write for a little while.

I got your newspapers and some back letters to the address while at sea. About how many did you mail? I didn't get the box.

I am awful tired and am going to sleep now. So I'll close. I love you and am being careful.

Your son,

Tommy J.

P.S. You get mail so quick because you are a day behind us.

Jan. 17, Tuesday

Dear family,
You aren't going to believe where I am, because it is really a stupid place. Our platoon left the main area we were in and came way out in the jungles to a place where we can run some patrols on an area. It is just an outpost to spend the time when we are not in the field.

The camp is a grave-yard, in the middle of a rice paddy. They have big old tombs and we have put shelters over them and are living there.

We have built some huts out of straw and bamboo also. There are 7 different posts and a main post for the leaders in our camp. They split the platoon up and when we are not on a patrol or something we stand guard in these posts. Someone has to be at a post at all times. The two platoons before us that lost some men, from mines and booby traps, were out here. We lost one Monday when he hit a mine. He hit his legs mostly. This whole area is all booby traps. They want to secure this area from patrols, because there are not many V.C., just traps. We go out for the first time in the morning. We have to run an ambush. I will really be shaking.

The squad leader just killed a gigantic rat. He was trying to steal our straw in our hut. Ha Ha.

I just got through making me a bed, or at least I call it a bed. I used bamboo and straw. It is not home style, but it is the best I could do. Well I guess I will eat my wonderful "C" rations. That is all we get out here. They do bring mail in and out. We will be here about 10 days.

I'll write more later.

Tuesday evening

I know Kaye's birthday is coming up on Feb. 7, but I can't buy anything over here.

If it wouldn't be to much trouble, I would sure appreciate you buying something nice for her and wrap it up for me. Please take the money out of my account. That is the only way it would really be from me. I'll be sending home some money as soon as we get paid in Feb. Let me know if you start getting the allotment check for $60. Also let me know about the bonds.

Well I have to get up early in the morning so I will close.

Love

Your son,

Tommy J.

P.S. I got the socks and Kool-aid - Thanks heaps!

Jan. 24, 67

Dear Mother & Daddy,
This check is a reimbursement for extra travel pay I was to get. I don't know why but I am not arguing. I signed it and you can put it into my account. I'll be sending a $50 check as soon as we get paid. Also you should get $60 allotment check. They owe me a lot of back pay, but they say I'll get it soon.

I got letters last night from Mr. & Mrs. Hogan, Steve Hogan, and Tommy Neal, and also Mrs. Bowman. The mail is doing O.K. now.

I'll close till later. I love you all.

Sorry to hear about Johnny's leg. I know it will really be a hinder to him.*

Tommy J.
You have to sign this check also when you cash it.

January 24, 67

Dear family,
The pictures turned out pretty good. I am sending back all except the ones of home. Split them up between you and Kaye. I am sending some more soon. They will be one more pack of black & white and then I'm going to buy color film.

We are now back at Battallion headquarters staging our company to go on the operation. It is going to be really rough, because there is nothing where we are going except V.C. We have to build a place to stay. We will leave in about a week.

I have good news. Every man in my squad got an appreciation letter from a big General over here for getting all those V.C. They were real important and had important papers. The letter goes in our record book. Good start.

---

* Tommy's younger brother Johnny had broken his leg during a soccer game at O'Keefe High School.

One of the boys who got shot the other day died this morning. It was real bad. Another is getting discharged.

I got the box you sent and a lot of letters today. Even a letter from the Hogan's and one from Tommy Neal. I can't catch up on letters — I can't find time. Maybe I will catch up soon. If my letters are slack the next few months, don't worry because I don't think we will have much time. I know you understand.

Well I'll close for now and let you know what's happening later.

Your son,

Tommy J.

January 24, 1967

Dear Mr. & Mrs. Hogan,

I received your letter and was real glad to hear from you. All my friends are being real thoughtful and it makes me feel real good.

We are in a preparation period right now to go on a big operation. We will go South of Danang to a valley [Que Son] *which is suppose to be a Viet Cong supply route. It also may be a collection point for the V.C. Only our company is going and that will make it hard if we find very many Viet Cong. But they are suppose to have a Regiment on stand-by if we need them. We will leave for there in a week or so.*

I hope Mike makes good in his school and I hope he can get a good duty station after he gets out. This is no place for anybody. I hope it can end soon. I am glad Pat is doing good in school. He can really go far I know.

We had a formation today and each man in my squad received a citation from a General here for killing 4 Communist V. Cong and capturing one who were top men. They had important papers on them. We also got some weapons. The citation went on our record and will help us later on for promotions.

Well I will close for now. Tell the whole family hello for me. I was glad to hear about those children of Steve's. Looks like one will be some basketball player.

Tommy

Jan. 27, 67

Dear family,
Last night I got the box of articles I asked for. Thank you heaps for it. I hope it wasn't any trouble. I also got a goodie package from the Bowman's. They sure are being great. They are just like a second family. I also received a letter from a Mrs. Betty McClure [a neighbor]. *She wrote a couple of verses and it was just what I had been looking for. 1 Peter 2:13*. It's about obeying man's law. So me being here is man's will and I have to abide. I wrote her a letter thanking her. She said she was your next door neighbors daughter.*

We got word we will be pulling out tomorrow (Jan. 28). I don't know what to expect. I was made automatic rifleman of my squad now. I'll make a couple of pictures in combat gear for you.

Letters might come slow now because the only way we can get anything out there is by helecopter. I don't know how often they will come. I got another request to ask. In your next package please send a pair of cut off blue jeans or some kind of shorts to wear around the area when we are not on duty. It is getting awful hot and I might as well get a tan. At least get use to the heat. I doubt if I will have that much leisure time but if nothing else, I'll sleep in them. They don't have to be blue jeans. Any kind of solid or dark colored shorts.

I know it is hard for you to send so many packages and letters. So I will understand if you cut down to occasional. I am here for a long time and that could get expensive.

Well I have to get my gear ready to go so I will close.

Be good. Your son,

Tommy J.

P.S. I sure was sorry to hear about Johnny's leg. I hope it won't be a handicap to him. He is a veteran athlete. The reason I needed most of those supplies was to clean my weapon. The lighter fluid will take off rust. If that don't work I use the steel wool. Don't worry, I haven't started smoking yet.

---

* The passage Betty McClure sent was: "Submit yourselves to every ordinance of man for the Lord's sake..." —1 Peter, Chapter 2, Verse 13

January 29, 1967

Hello College Kid Hogan,
I hope you are getting your Psychology down pat. It really sounds like fun. I am really having a ball on my free vacation. It is real hot now and I am getting real tan this early in the year.

Right now I am waiting on helecopters to pick us up and move us down to the new location I told you about. It is between Danang and Chu Lai on a Mountain called "Hill 185." Sounds war-like don't it. We are suppose to stop all V.C. supply routes around there. It is going to be a big job. You will probably read about the 1st Marines, Foxtrot Co.

I was made an automatic rifleman now. I really look bad. My weapon will put out 700 rounds per minute. A lot of lead, right.

Don't worry about my health. Unless the V.C. have my name on a bullet, I'll be O.K. I don't think they can spell my name.

I heard about the Super Bowl game in the newspaper. I bet it was good. I got a letter from your parents and also Steve [Hogan]. *I was glad they wrote.*

I guess you still have your long hair. One of the girl-killer looks. Well I'll close now and mail this. Be good and have fun. I don't guess you can do both.

Your pal,

Tommy J.

Tommy J.'s military gear.

"I'll make a couple of pictures in combat gear for you."

Hill 185 Nui Loc Son

CHAPTER FIVE

In late February 1967, units of the 3rd and 21st VC regiments, part of the 2nd NVA Division, arrived in the Que Son Valley in force. The battle for control of the valley was just beginning, With the increase in troops, F Company stayed busy patrolling the valley, determined to keep the VC and NVA from using it as a supply route. Most of the Company's skirmishes went their way, however, and the Marines did not believe for a minute that they were in danger of being outnumbered. In every encounter, the V.C. body count was high. "I don't see how the V.C. get their will to fight," Tommy would soon write home. "They are surely losing all the war."

OPPOSITE: Tommy J., second from left, with fellow marines. RIGHT: Tommy J., left, clowning around with another marine.

Feb. 2, 67

Dear family,
I am finally on the mountain. I did a lot before I got here and saw a lot of things I sure didn't want to see. When our platoon was getting ready to leave the area, our squad was called up to take a Major out to the field. It was operation "Sparrell-Hawk" [sic: Sparrow Hawk]. *After we got there we couldn't get back in, so we had to stay out there and finish up the operation with two other companies. We searched a whole area that was as big as Texas. Late Tuesday evening, we got hit with a 50 cal. machine gun ambush. It is the biggest machine gun the Marine Corps and the U.S. has. One Lieutenant from the other company got hit and he was killed. Then we began to open up. They called for artillery support and it blew a village completely away. We had to go in and I saw the worse sight I have ever seen. The whole village, including people, children, and animals, were blown all to pieces. We finally ended the operation and came back in.*

Yesterday, we finally got helecoptered to the mountain.

Talk about living conditions, this place beats all. It really has a lot of work to be put into it. The mountain sits right at the mouth of a deep valley which runs all the way to Cambodia. We have got to stop all V.C. action. Yesterday, 1st platoon got one man killed while running a patrol. Today, two squads of our platoon ran another patrol. My squad didn't have to go. They got into action and think they got 3 V.C. This place is really full of them.

We will work awful hard for about a month trying to get a place to live. I don't know how long we will be here, but it is a long time to live on "C" rations and no showers and in foxholes. But things just go that way. One day this will all be a dream, but I hope I don't dream about it. I can sure use those goodie packages these next few months. Also put a couple of writing pens in one package for me. I hope I am not asking to much of you to send things. If so just tell me. I can get along good enough to survive.

I hope you are all well. I hope Johnny's leg is not giving him any trouble.

Well it's about time for me to start working again so I will close. Say hello to everyone.

Your son,

Tommy J.

Sunday, Feb. 5

Dear family,
I hope this will find you all well. I am O.K. and nothing much has happened to me. My squad was moved from the big mountain to another small hill for 3 days. The South Viet army controls it, but they won't stay there unless they have some Marines with them. We will go back in the morning and somebody else will come out. The other platoons have been receiving a lot of action on their patrols. One platoon today had 3 wounded.

Boy is it hot. I have already blistered, peeled, and starting to tan pretty good. It only takes a couple of hours to blister bad. I have quit wearing underwear and a shirt most of the time. I wear a T-shirt sometimes. It is still cool at night.

I got paid yesterday and I am sending home some of this $50 check. I hope you get it and the $60 allotment check. Did you get the $30 check also I sent earlier?

I am really feeling like a tramp. I don't get time to shave or take a bath. I can only wash from a canteen.

Well in 2 more days I will have 2 months overseas duty completed. It has not gone by too slow. But of course there is not much time to get bored.

In any future packages, you had better be careful of things melting. I like things like canned fruit and canned goods I can eat instead of "C" rations. Also some goodies. I am not telling you to send them, those are just suggestions.

Well I will close for now. I hope everything is alright at home. I think of it often. The house sounds like it is shaping up. I hope Johnny has mastered his handicap. Tell him not to worry because he can't drive for awhile; I also miss it.

Your son,

Tommy J.

Feb. 8, 67

Dear folks,
I was glad to get a few letters from you today. I also got a package from the Bowmans. It sure hit the spot, taking the place of "C" rations.

I got 2 newspapers the other day. They were addressed to the old address while on ship. I hope you have changed it, or it will take longer. I must admit I don't have time to read it completely, but I scan the important parts.

I have caught a small cold from the hot days and cool nights on the mountain. I guess I'll go see the corpsman.

We have been out on a all day and night patrol today. It sure is tiring lugging these mountains.

This part of the country is so strange and spooky. The V.C. here are more powerful than where I used to be. Nobody has messed with them and it will take us awhile to get them under control, but I guarantee we will. The sooner we do, the sooner I come home.

I guess Jean and them got settled O.K. I haven't heard for awhile. She asked me if I wanted her to bake me a cake. I said yes but I think I should have not done it so soon after their move. I hope it won't set her back. I guess I am taking advantage of people wanting to send things. The Hogan's and Pat also said they had sent packages.

Castle in the Sands

Are the neighbors complaining about the wood piling up in the yard? I hope not. Tell Daddy not to work real hard. I would like to have a hand in building some nice places. I am learning a pretty good bit here. I have to build everything I need. Now we live in a sandbag bunker with rubber floats for beds. We call it the "Castle in the Sands." Ha Ha.

Did Johnny make "Red Rose Ball" candidate this year? I hope so.

Well I guess that is about all. You said if I got too much mail you would quit writing. You could never send too much mail. I am not a boot marine anymore. Probably before June I will have made Lance Corporal. They say I am doing a good job.

We lost one other boy from our platoon when a mortar bomb exploded. It blew out his eye. I sure hated for that to happen because he was a real good Marine and only had a few months left over here.

Be good. Don't worry.

Tommy J.

Feb. 11

Dear Mom & Pop Davis,
We are now located on a mountain top South of Danang. We carry out a search and destroy from here. The mountain sits right at the mouth of a big valley which the V.C. use for bringing in supplies and men. Our company is suppose to stop them from coming in. It is a big job going up and down this mountain all the time, especially since it has turned hot.

The living conditions on this mountain aren't very good either. We have to build it up a lot before we can be comfortable.

I hope your weather has gotten better. I guess it is still pretty cold there.

I am now on my 3rd month overseas duty. Time is going by pretty fast for me. I hope it just keeps it up. I should be home before next Christmas if everything goes right. If the war is not over, I could be extended or have a second tour over here. I just hope not.

Well I will close for now. Tell everyone hello for me.

Tommy J.

February 16, 1967

Hello Pat,
I hope this finds you doing well. I got your letter the other day but I am just now getting to answer it. We have been having a lot of action but it isn't going our way. My platoon went out last week and we got ambushed by a large force of V.C. They dropped mortar bombs into our position and we received 20 wounded-in-actions. I had to be one of them. I got a cut across my shoulder from a piece of metal that shoots from the mortar. We had 4 serious wounded who had to be hospitalized. I am O.K. and the wound is healing fine. It healed so fast, I start going back out tomorrow.

The V.C. are starting to put up a big fight, because they know they are losing. We got to pile it on them now.

We got a big treat today. They brought in ice to the mountain and I mixed up some Kool-aid and had a real cold drink. I guess that sounds stupid to you but it was something great to me.

I was sorry to hear Russell joined the Corps. Especially since it is for 4 years. I don't think he will like it, because I sure as hell know I don't. I miss home like something awful. I even miss WQXI radio. This hole in the ground sucks. I would have to turn to this page [Stationary heading: SMILE: Thing's couldn't possibly get worse!]

I guess your basketball is about over. I hope you won the rest of them.

I got a valentine card from your family. It got here right on time. That was good timing.

Well I will close for now. Either be good or have fun.

Your pal,

Tommy J.

Tommy J. and his platoon climbing the mountain.

"Foxtrot"

Part of Revolutionary Development Plan

Col. Radics' 'baby battalion'

By: SSgt Jack "W" Jansen and
Cpl Lowell L. Carson

DA NANG—During January the First Marine Regiment assumed the additional responsibilities of taking over the Nui Loc Son outpost, some 30 miles south of Da Nang, in the Hiep Duc and Que Son valleys.

Infantrymen of "F" Company, 2nd Battalion, First Marine Regiment; artillerymen of "W" Battery, 1st Battalion, 11th Marine Regiment; engineers and a helicopter support team (HST), are the Marines manning the outpost.

These Marines are what is known by the 1st Marines as a "baby battalion" or, as Colonel Emil J. Radics, commanding officer of the Regiment says, "They are my 4th Battalion."

"Nui Loc Son is one of several locations in the I Corps area that have recently been taken over by the Marines," said Colonel Radics. "It was necessitated by the decision of the I Corps commanders that Vietnamese troops should work basically in the Revolutionary Development Plan. That meant working with the people instead of being operational against the Viet Cong," he said.

When word came to the First Marines that they would take over operations of Nui Loc Son, the regimental command post took on the aspects of an "aggravated bee hive."

One heavily reinforced company with supplies for five days was the initial order. Radics soon changed that to a minimum of 15 days supplies.

"I don't want to have to start worrying about those men if the weather holds up resupply runs for a week. Now I know they have enough food and ammunition for a two week period," he said.

It became the job of Major Howard L. Snider, air liaison officer for the regiment, to obtain helicopter and fixed wing support for Nui Loc Son.

"Without air there would be no Nui Loc Son," he said. "The only way supplies can be delivered is by air."

The pilots who started the build up had to maneuver their helicopters between rocks onto an improvised landing zone. Within a month the engineers had blasted the rocks out and constructed a prefabricated landing zone on the hill.

On Jan. 31, the first of the Marines landed on the mountain. For four days after the initial lift choppers were grounded because of adverse weather. They made up for the lull by delivering 100,000 pounds of supplies the fifth day.

"Since that time," said Major James L. Gatliff, logistics officer for the regiment, "We've had 155 air lifts averaging 15,000 pounds a day."

During the first days of the move nearly every helicopter came under fire from the Viet Cong. Marine air and artillery were used to silence the enemy in the valley.

During the daylight hours Marines of "F" Co., tore down old bunkers and began building new ones. They dug trench lines and increased the sanitary conditions.

Engineers destroyed mine fields and constructed the landing zone for the choppers. From early morning until dusk the helicopter support team guided in choppers and unloaded supplies.

At night all Marines stood guard on the perimeter, rounding out a long day's work.

Now the Marines have lived on Nui Loc Son for over a month. They have torn down the old and built the new. "An outpost acceptable to Marines for defense," says Colonel Radics.

The Marines must now begin their second and biggest job at the outpost. They must observe, control and eliminate the enemy in the populated, rice-rich area surrounding Nui Loc Son.

They have already begun accomplishing this mission through civic action for the people and hard fought battles with the enemy.

Leathernecks at Nui Loc Son carry on the Marine Corps' "double barrel" attack against the Viet Cong day and night. "It is through this type action," says Colonel Radics, "that this enemy will be eventually defeated."

4 SEA TIGER

An article featuring Tommy J.'s Regiment, that appeared in the *Sea Tiger*

Feb. 22

Dear family,
Well more big news to tell, if you hadn't already read about it. We had a report of 10 V.C. which had been going into a certain village for a couple of nights straight. So our commander picked a 15 man killer team to go out and set up an ambush. I got picked to go. We had to be extremely quiet and careful, because with only 15 men, you could easily get overrun. We set in at our sight and waited. About 7 a.m. (Feb. 20) we heard voices coming. We begin to look and then I couldn't believe my eyes. All kind of V.C. with weapons coming across a rice paddy toward us. They were completely unaware of us being there. They estimated about 50 or 60 V.C. with 2 other platoons of them about 1/2 mile behind. It was a whole company. We waited till their first man was about 5 feet in front of our position and then we opened up with everything we had. Only 15 guys shooting away at a platoon. They began falling everywhere. They tried to shoot back but we were too much for them. The rear of them turned into a tree-line and were running like scared rabbits. They tried to pull off some wounded and others crawled off. We had, after the shooting stopped, 12 dead KIA [killed in action] V.C. and 2 WIA [wounded in action] V.C. with 12 weapons. When our commanding officer heard of our success, he brought the whole company down to support us. Artillery hit in the spot where they fled and also air strikes came. The air strikes got an estimated 25 V.C.

I went out with the first 4 men to pick up weapons and see if wounded were left. They were North VietNam's Hard Corps: all young boys. We really put it to them. The General came out to shake our hand later that day.

Our whole company has had good luck. For the last 3 days we have killed 21 V.C. and captured 4 wounded. Also we have gotten 20 weapons. Is that enough excitement?

I am O.K. and doing fine. I hope you are well. I'll have to close now, but I'll write more later.

Your son,

Tommy J.

Top: Base Camp
Bottom: Tommy J.'s tent

Feb. 23

Dear family,
Just a few lines to let you know I am O.K. I just got a package from the Bowman's today. It was real good.

They have changed our address again. Maybe this is why I haven't been getting my mail as soon as I should. Tell Jean about it and also Pat Hogan if you see him before I write.

Did I tell you the Hogan's sent me a big box of homemade cookies? Boy were they good.

We went out again today and killed 3 V.C. snipers. We are really putting it to them now. Company has 21 killed and about 5 or 6 captured this week only.

I had to be put on no duty for a couple of days today. I have an infected foot around my ankle. It is from walking in the rice paddy's and water all day. It should be O.K. soon. I can't wear a boot on that foot for awhile.*

I hope all is well there. I must close now. Just wanted to get you this address.

PFC T.J. Holtzclaw, 2277708
H.Q. 1st Marine Reg.
"F" Co. 2nd Plat.
c/o FPO San Francisco, Calif. 96602

February 24, 1967

Hello Pat,
I hope this finds you getting well educated. I am learning all kinds of things also. How to fill sandbags, how to walk a lot, how to duck bullets, how to be miserable and all that good stuff. Wouldn't you love to learn that? You are crazy if you do.

---

* Tropical immersion foot was a common problem among the American soldiers in Vietnam. It was the result of standing or walking for prolonged periods in rice paddy water, aggravated by the heat and humidity of the jungle. Advanced immersion foot often involved blisters and open sores, which led to fungal infections. In such cases, immersion foot was sometimes referred to as "jungle rot."

It is not really that bad. It is just the homesickness that is bad. At the end of this month I'll be going into my 4th month of overseas duty. It is going by pretty fast. We have really been having some good hunting lately. Our platoon has killed 13 V.C. and wounded 2 captives in the last week. The company has 21 altogether so we are beginning to kick ass since I wrote you last. I don't see how the V.C. get their will to fight. They are surely losing all the war.

Boy is it hot here now. Hotter than Atlanta ever gets. Summers don't even start till June. Humping this mountain doesn't help matters any either.

I have a new address now also. My mail has really been messed up. Maybe this will straighten it out. It is:

PFC T.J. Holtzclaw, 2277708
H.Q. 1st Marine Reg.
Fox Company, 2nd Platoon
c/o FPS San Francisco, Calif. 96602

Well I will close for now. Take it easy and study hard, pal. Thanks for writing.

Your ole pal,

Tommy

Feb. 26

Dear family,
I received 2 packages from you last night in the mail. I am in the process of consuming the goods now. It sure is good. Thanks alot. I also got the pictures; marked what they were on the back and am sending them back home. The newspaper order came also in the mail. You won't have to take out another subscription, because they don't get here. I only received 2 and you shouldn't be wasting your money on that. We usually get a small paper printed in Okinawa.

Nothing much has happened since my last letter.

We went out this morning, but nothing happened. We only received a few sniper rounds.

I am also sending an example of how my correct address should be. Maybe I'll get it straight sooner or later.

I got a letter from Mom Davis and also Monroe Davis [Tommy's uncle on his mother's side]. *That was a surprise.*

I am glad Johnny won. I figured he would. I only wish I could have been there to take Kaye. I know it must have been awful hard to see everybody else with a date and her alone. But I just couldn't do it.*

Now that I know what a bigger war this is than people think, I am glad I am here.

Some of the boys are married with two or more children. So I know it is worse for them. I just wish people back there who riot and have demonstrations could see what it is like and give us some support instead of trouble. That would help the cause a lot.

I wrote Rev. Luckett a letter a week or so ago. I wonder if he got it? I hope your finger is well, mother, and I hope Johnny's leg is getting better.

I must close now. Will write again soon.

Tommy J.

Feb. 27

Dear family,
I received your letter today that you were worried about my wound. I am sorry I haven't said more about it, I started not to even write about it. I hope you didn't get one of those scary telegrams. I requested you not. The wound was just a small gash across the shoulder about one inch. I had 3 spaced stitches in it just to hold it together and make it heal fast. Now, I can just barely see a scar. We were all put up for purple hearts. But after I had written the letter they found out that what went off was one of our own grenades. A boy had it on his rifle and a bullet must have hit it,

* O'Keefe High School's Dance Club hosted the Red Rose Ball each year. Johnny Holtzclaw was voted "court representative" for his class.

causing it to go off. They really don't know if that was it or not, but the grenade was missing and the boy didn't shoot it. He also got wounded. But, because it was said to be friendly forces mistake, no purple hearts. I don't want one anyway. I just want to go home without that medal. But don't worry about that wound. I am now back on full duty.
It is raining today, but it will probably clear up.

We got some good news today. They are starting to send about 18 men every 3 days to a place near Danang called "China Beach" for rest. Since we have to live on "C" rations and under these living conditions they let us go for a couple of days to eat hot meals and take showers, and just rest. We sent 2 today. I don't know when I will go, but I am sure looking forward to it. It will have to be before the next month is up.

Well I will close for now. Just didn't want you to worry. Tell Johnny I received his letter and will try to answer it soon.

Tommy J.

Life on the Mountain

CHAPTER SIX

On top of Nui Loc Son, life for the Marines of Fox Company improved. They settled into bunkers they'd built, enjoyed freshly cooked meals flown in (some of them Vietnamese), and even managed to bring along a record player so they could enjoy the same music they'd been listening to at home: the Rolling Stones, the Monkees, James Brown and the Supremes. Despite those comforts, they were still at war. Patrols, ambushes and even trips to the newly established village below to conduct friendly pacification efforts continued to be risky and often met with casualties.

The principal enemy force in the Que Son basin were not really the V.C. Tommy wrote about. Instead, they were hardened regulars of the North Vietnamese Army, the 2nd NVA Division. Units of its 3rd and 21st Regiments arrived in force in late February 1967. As the year progressed, the 3rd VC Regiment, also part of the 2nd NVA Division, joined them. Intelligence picked up by the U.S. military suggested that the NVA were amassing troops to mount an attack.

Tommy J., confident that the Marines were "beating back" the Viet Cong, was hoping to soon get a break from the endless round of patrols and ambushes by being sent to a new R&R spot: China Beach. He wrote repeatedly about his hope to be sent there before the end of March. The beach lay east of Da Nang on the South China Sea, and gained its reputation after thousands of G.I.'s spent their leave there, surfing, holding barbecues, sunning on the white sands and enjoying a much-needed break from the war. The resortlike area was immortalized in a scene from the 1979 film *Apocalypse Now* showing a soldier surfing in front of a village under attack, and a decade later inspired the popular television series "China Beach."

While he waited his turn, Tommy fought the V.C. and counted down the months to the day his year would be up.

Left to right, Lonnie Matthews and Tommy J. on Nui Loc Son at the entrance to one of the bunkers they built.

March 1, 1967

Hi Pat,
I hope you are doing O.K. I am fine, except for a little homesickness. It has been bad the last couple of days. I keep remembering how much fun I had last year around this time.

I am fixing to go into my 4th month of this tour. It is ticking off slowly. I just wish I could set up the clock a bit.

We have been building on our living positions since we have been on the mountain. We have about 4 men to a position. Each position has to be made of sandbags about 2 or 3 wide. Then you just have to do the best you can about comforts We have built some wooden beds, made a small table and chair, and put up a few pictures (Playboy type). We use our candles for light and we even have a mouse trap to catch our pest. Some of those rats are so big, they'll carry it away if you don't tie it down.

Should be getting warm there soon. Then the "spring fever." That won't help your "C" average much.

Well since news is short, I will close this episode till later. Get on the books and pull in some knowledge.

By the way, do you know where Charles Wolraven went to be stationed? I sure would like to see him. We just got to have a reunion in about a year or so.

Be careful and write when you can.

Your ole pal,

Tommy

March 2, 67

Dear Mother,
Enclosed is this months check I am sending home. It is for $225.00. You should get the $60.00 check soon. Please let me know if these checks arrive O.K. Also tell me about how much I have in the bank now. I'll write a letter later. Thanks.

Tommy J.

March 4, 67

Dear Mother,
This is just a little letter to wish you a very "Happy Birthday" on March 10th. I feel real bad because I can't get you something, or even a card. So I hope this letter will be O.K. till I can get to somewhere I can buy things. I don't want you to worry about me, because it won't do any good. So let me handle my part over here and you just enjoy life.

Maybe Daddy and Johnny will take you out to eat like they should, because it will perturb me if they don't!

I hope everything around there is O.K.

I got some good news. They are letting different people from the company, who have been on the mountain the whole time, go into an area close to Danang called "China Beach" for 2 days of rest and recover. We send a couple of boys every 4 or 5 days. I am on our list to go real soon. It should be within the next 2 weeks. The beach is well protected and has a snack bar, a P.X., a beach for sunning and a recreational club. So I am looking forward to going.

Well I will close because we are going out tonight. I have to get my gear ready.

Happy Birthday again.

Your loving son,

Tommy J.

March 7, Tuesday

Dear folks,
I hope this finds you well. I am doing O.K. We have been working extra hard on the mountain getting it built up. Intelligence says the V.C. are regrouping to try and over run our position. We don't think they can do it. I don't even think they are planning it.

We heard from news that there are a large amount of Red Chinese now grouping around the DMZ. Have you heard any talk or news like that. I sure hope they aren't wanting to get in the action, because that will start big trouble.

I am now O.K. and no more no duty. My buddy (the one that is writing Brenda) informed me today that he was writing a letter telling you or Brenda that I didn't get wounded; because I got mad when he told me he wrote about it. I didn't want him to write, so he wrote a letter saying it wasn't really me but it was him. He thought I hadn't told you yet. I have already told you so it doesn't matter. Just wanted you to know what was going on if you got his letter. He also got wounded that day.

We have an operation coming up soon. I don't know much about it, but I'll write later.

I got your package with film and things in it. Thanks a lot. Did I tell you I received Mrs. McClure's package. It was very nice. I also got a couple from Mrs. Bowman.

Mrs. Hogan sent me some cookies, so you can see I am being well stocked.

Also, they have now started giving us two hot meals a day. They brought in cooks and stuff and they fly us food for each day. It sure is good. Beats "C" rations.

Tell Daddy that we have 2 Vietnamese barbers who came up the mountain to cut our hair. They use handclippers and it is quite different from his haircuts. But it keeps the hair from getting too long.*

Well, I guess that is all the news for now. I will write again soon.

Tommy J.

P.S. What did the news say about our ambush you heard on T.V.? We like to be heard about, ourselves.

P.S.S. We just got another mail call. Don't worry I am getting your mail now. We found this clipping in a paper that they distribute over here. That is our platoon and according to the way we go out all the time, I should be 3rd from the bottom. I can't tell much.

The other picture is a guy on the hill. The one with 3 words.

"There's a long, long trail a winding"

Elements of the 2d Bn., First Marine Regiment, 1stMarDiv., near the end of an exhausting climb to the summit of a mountain 30 miles southwest of Da Nang, where the unit has established a new base. (Photo by PFC Clark D. Thomas)

A photograph from an unidentified newspaper showing Tommy J.'s Regiment climbing the mountain.

* Tommy's mother was a part-time hairdresser who ran a salon out of her basement. Her husband T. J. also cut hair.

Tommy J. on Nui Loc Son

March 9, 67

Dear folks,
It has been raining all day and we couldn't do much. I think we will go out tonight, they haven't passed the word yet. If we do, it will be wet and miserable.

I'll be wearing 2 extra medals when I come home. The 1st Division was put up for one Navy Citation, and our 2nd Bn. was put up for a Presidential Citation. That means I have 4 medals from over here so far. 2 are given for being in Viet Nam. Including the National Defense Medal, I will have 5. I also have one battle star for being in Operation

"Sparrel-Hawk." [sic: Sparrow Hawk] *That is a good start I think.*

You ask me about a tape recorder or record player.

A tape wouldn't do any good because I don't have any time to talk. A record player would be nice because I love music, but we don't have electricity and a battery-type costs a lot. And it would be a lot of trouble sending all the records and albums all the time. Some boys have one and I listen to them sometimes. It would probably be hard to keep it up. Just tell Johnny to tell you the top ten now and write what they are. I am still a civilian at heart.

Well I am now into my 4th month overseas. How is that? Only 10 left. That don't sound so bad. It is better than when I was still at ITR [Infantry Training Regiment: The School of Infantry at Camp Lejeune, N.C.] *waiting to come over here.*

Well tomorrow will be Mother's Birthday. I sure hope you have a happy one, just for me. Happy Birthday!!

I guess you were surprised when I sent home that big check, weren't you? I told you I was going to save for big plans.

Well I will close since there is no news. Be good and don't worry.

I love you all.

Tommy J.

P.S. We won't go out till tomorrow. That is good!

Few Jokes for the week.

1. *"Where are we going to eat?"*
   "Let's eat up the street."
   "Naw, I hate asphalt."

2. *What the Doctors scribble on prescriptions to drugists!*
   "I've got my $10 - now he's all yours!"

3. *So the story goes, after the dragon finished eating Sir Lancelot, he said, "Tender is the knight"*

4. *Roger: "I thought the doctor told you to stop all drinks?"*
   Bill: "Well, you don't see any getting past me, do you?"

March 9, 67

Dear Mr. & Mrs. Hogan,
I hope this finds you doing well. I am doing fine. I received the box of cookies you sent last week. They were sure good.

They have now started giving us 2 hot meals a day here. They fly in the food each day and we have some cooks here which heat it up. It sure is better than "C" rations all the time.

Mother tells me the weather there is awful cold. I wish I could let you have some of our heat. We have enough for the both of us.

Our platoon all chipped in and we bought us a pet monkey. You should see some of the times we have with him. He is really a little devil. Sometimes he acts human and everyone gets a kick out of him. It gives you a little pleasure to kid around with him. His name is Dinky-Do.

I sure hope Mike makes it home for Easter. Does he know how long his schooling is for?

Our whole Company is supposed to get a new kind of rifle before the end of this month. The army has already adopted it and now we are suppose to get it. It looks like a Space Gun or something. It is called the M-16. It is suppose to be a much better weapon.*

Well I had better close now. I have to write a couple of other people. Thanks again for the packages and letters.

Your friend always,

Tommy Holtzclaw

---

* The original M-16 rifles were considered by many to be more deadly than the enemy. The new gun was sensitive and required endless maintenance, and in the humid jungle climate, was notoriously unreliable, and soldiers often had little or no time to become familiar with it Soldiers were warned to make sure that the chambers of the rifles were very clean. Under combat conditions the M16 had a tendency to malfunction. It often jammed after firing several rounds, due to a stuck round in the chamber. To clear the rifle, the cleaning rod had to be assembled and poked through its barrel.. Its suitability for use in a tropical climate was never taken into account. M-16s were soon referred to as "Mattel Toys" or "widowmakers." Though the new rifles were on the way, F Company continued to use their M-14s throughout the month of March.

March 15, 1967

Hi Pat,
I hope this finds you passing everything. Don't let spring fever get a hold on you. We by-passed spring here. Summer heat came in one day. I am glad I came when I did and can get use to it before the really hot months get here. I pity the boys coming over around June or July.

Right now we are on an outpost from our mountain. It is a small hill about a mile from the mountain. Our squad is here for 4 days and then another squad will come over. The hill has South Viet soldiers on it, but they won't stay unless some Marines are here at all times. We are their heroes. Ha.

If you are liked by the people over here, they call you No. 1, if you aren't liked you are called No. 10. Not many are brave enough to call you No. 10!

We had more action 2 days ago. Our platoon went out on an ambush and we came upon some V.C. sleeping in a hut. We killed 2, wounded 2 and captured a woman V.C. We also got 3 weapons. After we had collected the weapons we were about to leave the site. We had just walked into an open rice paddy and I was 2nd man in the column. About 4 of us had entered the clearing when heavy automatic fire opened up on us and pinned 3 of us down in the paddy. We couldn't get up because the rounds were hitting all over. They kept us there about 10 minutes, then we just got up and ran back to cover. I was sure scared. Then we opened up on the area and they fled. In all we had a good day.

Well, I am sure going to miss not going to Spivey this year. All this good tan and nobody to show it to.*

Kaye and I are still pretty serious. She is being true and maybe she will wait. I hope so.

Glad to hear Mike got home. I know he is anxious to come visit me. Ha.

Your folks sure have been great. They write plenty of letters and also send packages. I sure do appreciate it.

Well I will close this time. Be good and study hard.

Your pal,

Tommy

---

* From 1959 to 1969, Atlanta's Lake Spivey was known as the world's largest man-made beach. Its two-miles of sand had public docks, bathhouses and a pavilion. and was a popular teen hot spot in the '60s, the site of "Beach Hops" that featured concerts with live bands. Tommy J. had been a frequent visitor.

March 16, 67

Dear Poppa-Son, Mommy-Son, and Brother-son,
(Vietnamese for Daddy, Mother, and Johnny)

I hope this finds you at the peak of relaxation and are happy. I am doing fine. Number one son just finish eating chop-chop (food). Roast-beef, potatoes, pork & beans, fruit cocktail and Cherry Kool-aid. The last 3 were from packages.

We have been at the outpost (the one that is manned by South Vietnamese) for 4 days. You remember we were there at the 1st of Feb. A squad out of the company goes every 4 days for security. I am glad our turn is over again. Those Vietnamese are crazy and funny. They really think a lot of Marines. When you are liked by these people, they call you Number one; if you aren't liked or you make them mad they call you Number Ten! If you want to taste a really different meal, eat with them once. Rice every meal topped with one of their sauces. Sometimes it's pretty good. Then after the meal, you get rice wine. Strong stuff! But nothing can beat American food.

Well, just before we went to the outpost we had another victory. Our platoon went on an ambush. Each squad went to different places. Our squad ran upon 2 V.C. and we killed one and wounded one and got 2 weapons. 1st squad killed one, wounded one and also got one weapon. Our squad also captured a woman V.C.

We moved all the villages in the surrounding area to one area just below our mountain. Now, anything out there is V.C. So it should be easier hunting. We are suppose to get relieved from the mountain in late April. Then we will go back either North of Danang or to the DMZ. I pray not the latter.

Instead of renewing the newspaper for me, I would rather receive some magazines every once in a while. They will have to be wrapped in brown paper, so nobody takes them. Maybe Look* *or* Sports Illustrated *or some good magazine. Just buy one and sent it, don't subscribe to one. Somebody got a* Life *today, I enjoyed it but I think* Look *is a better one.*

I got your package today and it sure was good, especially the fruit and Dr. Pepper.

---

* *Look* was a weekly, general-interest magazine published in the United States from 1937 to 1971. There was more of an emphasis on photographs than articles.

We got a new squad leader and he seems to be O.K. We go out tonight so we will see.

I am glad my money is building up. If you need money at any time, please take it out and use it. That would make me happy to know I could help. I want Mother to take out $15.00 or ever how much it costs to buy her an Easter Dress. Don't say no, because it would really disappoint me. After you get it, you must get Kaye to take your picture in it so I will know you got it. Be sure and use my money, because I can't get it for you.

Well I must close now. Be good and don't worry.

No. one son,

Tommy J.

March 16

Hi John,

Hope this finds you walking O.K. now. I guess that was a big hinder to you. Glad O'Keefe did so well in soccer. Sure wish I could have played.

Well your 16th birthday is coming up and time for the big Driver's License. I hope you pass the test, don't run into any poles while watching the blinker. After you get them, you best be careful driving; especially in the Phantom.

I hope you have a happy birthday on Easter.

You don't have any of those join the service attitudes I hope. I might have to kick your butt if you try that. Take my word, you don't want in this thing. One fool in the family is enough. Just go to college and don't sign up unless you have to. Then only come in for the shortest time possible.

I guess you and Sharon are getting along O.K. Tell her she looked very nice for the Red Rose Ball.

Well just wanted to wish you a Happy Birthday! Be good.

Your brother,

Tommy J.

March 20, 67

Dear family,
Here is a picture of the V.C. weapons we took off the 12 dead V.C. we ambushed a couple of weeks ago. You can see we got a lot of them to be only an 11 man team. I am sitting in the corner and that is a real good picture of them. The one in the middle, a orange colored one, is Chinese made. That is a lot of gear that they won't use on us again.

Also, there are 2 negatives of a bunch of us sitting around and one of our bunkers we live in when it was almost finished.

You can have them developed into color pictures. I also sent home a roll of film. Send them back so I can see them, and then I'll return them.

Don't worry. I am O.K. I'll write more later.

Tommy J.

Confiscated V.C. weapons, the orange one is Chinese made

March 20

Dear Jean, J.C., Connie and Terri,
I received the nice package you sent me and it was greatly appreciated, I assure you. Thanks a lot.

The weather is quite hot now. Today was about 128! and the sun really takes out all my energy.

I sent home some more pictures today so maybe Mother will bring them sometime when she comes to see you.

Daddy said he is buying a hauling trailer to get lumber up to the lot and also he was looking at some trailers in Athens. I am glad he has something to do now and can get out for awhile. I just hope he doesn't hurt himself working too hard. I would really like to help him.

Our squad has a patrol tomorrow night and we are going quite a long way from our area. It will surely be spooky, plus I have to walk 2nd man from the front. This place can do a job on the nerves.

Soon it will be Easter and it is hard to believe. I guess the girls will be all prettied up. Maybe you will take a picture. Well, I must close for now and I'll write more later. Be Good.

Tommy J.

Tommy J.'s nieces left to right: Terri and Connie

March 22, 67

Dear family,
How is it going? Your little boy is doing just fine except for being lazy. These hot days don't let you do much, and then it still has to be done. I put in these clippings for you. The poems I thought were pretty good and I thought you might like the other one also. They came out of a small paper that is printed somewhere around here.

BOONDOCK BARDS

Stars and Stripes welcomes poetry from its readers. Contributions should be typed or block printed and double-spaced. Send them to Boondock Bards, Pacific Stars and Stripes, APO 96503. Editors reserve the right to reject or make minor changes. All contributions whether used or not become the property of Pacific Stars and Stripes. No poems will be returned and editors will not engage in correspondence about them.

A Letter to Parents

A boy is born in warmth and grace,
Two parents gaze upon his face.
In their eyes a priceless gem,
This new creation a part of them.
Their child, a boy with curly hair,
They raise him with the best of care.
And now at school, his parents wait,
To see their young son graduate.
You've raised him well so take your bow,
But "Uncle Sam," he wants him now.
So with induction worry starts,
They bid goodby with troubled hearts.
Yes, worry masked behind a grin,
They pray "Dear Lord, take care of him."
He breaks the news of Vietnam,
I'll be OK, don't worry Mom.
Aboard a ship with gun in hand,
He journeys to this far off land.
A land of strife, a land of war,
Their son is not a child anymore.
Within this land so ripped and torn,
A child has died, a man is born.

PFC A.H. Lauer
2d Bn., 39th Inf.

Once Civilians

We were once civilians, back in the States,
With our "Soupedup" Chevs and Saturday night dates.
Out every night looking for fun,
Not giving up till we could see the sun.
Then one day a letter came thru,
Saying, "Greetings . . . have picked you."
We weren't draft dodgers by any means,
Didn't start school or protest scenes.
We began basic training, green and new,
With graduation, the thing in view.
Advanced training was our next inclination,
Of how we would spend our obligation.
We received our orders, the picture was clear,
Southeast Asia would be home for a year.
Now we are soldiers, which we don't regret,
There is an enemy to fight, and we haven't won yet.
Someday we'll back with our Chevs and dates,
Feeling real proud we have served our States.

SP4 Bill Winger
PFC Vance Gervais
HHC, 10th Cbt Avn Bn

This is the column that Tommy J. mentioned in his letter. It appeared regularly in the Armed Services newspaper, *Pacific Stars and Stripes*. The column printed poetry written by American servicemen serving in Vietnam.

Last night our squad was suppose to go out by ourselves but intelligence called just before we went out and said we had better call it off; because they had reports that the V.C. had a large force in this area probably setting in an ambush for our patrol. So our whole platoon is going out tonight and we want to "kick tails and take names!" That is an expression for get the better of them. Good winning spirit I think. We know for sure that they are scared and now we want to play bully and we want to give them no slack. Last night a V.C. surrendered to us and he said others want to also surrender, but they couldn't get away from their officers. We are Bad news!

One of my buddies got a portable record player today from home, but we don't have any records to play on it. So I said I would see if you would buy me a few albums and send them. Use my money and get Johnny to make some good selections. Tell him to get these albums if he can:

1. *"The Best of the Animals" by The Animals*
2. *An album by the Rolling Stones - any good one.*
3. *A good one by The Supreme's*
4. *James Brown's Album that has "I Feel Good" on it*
5. *The Monkee's "I'm a Believer"*

And he can pick the rest. 45's will even do. Just make the package under 5 lbs. Use my money for them. If it is too much trouble forget it. Don't insure it, because it takes too long. Wrap them extra good. Thanks so much, but don't go out of your way.

Well I hope Johnny has a Happy Birthday. Are you planning to go see Mom & Pop Davis on their anniversary? Well I must close for now. Be good and don't work too hard.

Tommy

March 24, 67

Dear family,
I hope this finds you doing O.K. It is sure hot today, like all the others. It is hard to believe this heat – unless you are here.

I got some more combat news for you. Our platoon really had it all in out fighting yesterday. We set out around midnight and each squad was to set up a different ambush. Well "Victor Charlie" must have been expecting us. 1st squad ran right into a V.C. ambush and rounds were flying everywhere. They jumped into a ditch and nobody got hit. Our squad set up an ambush along a trail and waited. About 3:30 a.m. V.C. started coming toward us. There were around 6 of them. But one of our men got trigger happy and opened up too soon. They turned and got away, but a couple must have been wounded. Then we couldn't leave because it was still dark so we stayed till daylight. Before daylight, the V.C. had surrounded us waiting for us to move during the night. But they fled when daylight came. We regrouped with our platoon and headed back. But it was a long way back. We had firefights constantly and rounds were hitting all around. We had 2 wounded in the legs and had to have a Medivac. I carried 240 rounds of ammunition out with me and when I got back, I only had 30 rounds left. That is a lot of fighting to use that many. I was glad to get back on the mountain.

Well I guess Easter will be over when you get this letter. I bet we are out in the field that day.

Well I will close for now. By the way, I got a letter from Nette and Lloyd White [Tommy's aunt and uncle on his father's side], *but she didn't give me her address so I can't answer it. If you write her anytime soon let her know I got it.*

Be good.

Tommy

March 28, 1967

Dear family,
This letter should relieve you for a few days at least.

You remember my capped tooth that is unbreakable, well it got broke in two. I ran head on to another guy and his head hit right on the tooth. They are flying me out by helicopter in the morning and I am going back to the medical section of our headquarters to have it fixed. I am quite a sight right now and I am not much for eating. The dentist that gave me that tooth sure doesn't know his business. I am sort of mad and then again I'll be skating a couple of days.

We went out Easter morning and came back late in the afternoon. It figures we would be out, so that made Easter seem like any other day. I received the 2 packages from you. The one with the cake was mostly ruined because the cake had been busted on the side. The other was still good. I also got one from the Bowman's.

Boy is my hair ever turning grey. I am going to look like an old, old man. That worries me.

I haven't gone to the rest at China Beach yet. They have slacked up on sending us in, so I guess it will be awhile before I get to go.

By the time you get this letter, it will be 4 months completed overseas. Down to the single digit numbers now.

Well I hope there are no problems at home. I am doing enough fighting for the whole family, so everyone there should be getting along with each other. If you had rather fuss and fight, I'll gladly swap with you, because I think I'll be a very peace loving man now. You shouldn't make me have 2 worries on my mind.

Well I must close for now and will write more later.

Tommy

March 28, 1967

Hello Pat,
I hope this finds you O.K. I got to go into a Dentist at Headquarters tomorrow, because you remember my capped tooth, well I broke it in half again. I ran head onto another guy and his head caught me right in the mouth. So I get to skate a couple of days. But we are going out tonight and coming back in the morning; then I get helicoptered out. Tonight will be scary, because we run into action every time we go to this place. The V.C. are starting to set up ambushes. Our 1st squad got ambushed last time we went there which was five days ago. We will set up tonight along a main trail a good ways from here; then hope for the V.C. to come walking unexpectedly

down the trail. Then about a 340 burst of ammunition will open on them. That is the bad Marines! I hope it doesn't backfire.

You remember my grey hair? You should see it now. I bet I am completely grey before I am 21.

Well you lucky ass back in the world, with all the good food, booze, girl, somewhere to go and all the other stuff. Because you are such a good buddy, why don't you volunteer to come over here and relieve me so I can come home? That is not asking too much is it? Ha.

Well I guess I'll close for now and go down to the swimming pool for a while. And then again I might ride over and get a pizza at the local hangout.

Be bad and raise Hell!

Tommy J.

A Little Humor

Mother: "What would you like for Christmas, darling — a baby sister or brother?"

Darling: "Well, Mother, if you can carry the load, I'd rather have a pony."

March 31

Dear family,

Sure hope you are O.K. I got back from the Dentist today and he fixed all my teeth. He recapped my front tooth and filled my others. He filled the one the dentist in Atlanta wanted to pull. That perturbs me that my unbreakable cap broke! False Advertisement! My jaws are swollen up right now because he didn't cut me no slack with those shots. It was nice to be where I could take showers and eat at a real mess hall.

Our platoon captured a confirmed V.C. and he gave alot of information. He told how many V.C. are around here, how many weapons and ammunition, and even told of a training camp about a 2 day walk from here. He said the V.C. know every time we leave the mountain because they have warning devices. Our platoon has been ambushed twice now.

They have a new plan out, that whoever captures a live V.C. with weapons, gets a 5 day rest and recovery out of country. We get one after we have been here about 7 months and this one is extra. You can go to quite a few foreign countries: Japan, Phillipines, Hawaii, Thailand, China, Okinawa, Manila and others. That is a good benefit. One of my buddies captured one while I was at Headquarters so he will get to go.

The 3 days at China Beach, in country, is also given to us. We don't get to send as many men now, but I should go before too long.

I won't be sending home any money for a couple of months because I have to save it so I can go on R^est^ and R^ecover^. You will still get the $60.00 check. The clipping I am sending is a write up about us here on the Mountain. Pretty good. Save it.

Well I must close now. Be good.

Tommy J.

Almost Nineteen

CHAPTER SEVEN

Tommy's birthday was fast approaching—April 24th—and though he had not gotten his longed-for vacation at China Beach, he at least had some hope of making Lance Corporal in another month. On April 16, he observed the first anniversary of his relationship with his girlfriend Kaye, who had just turned 17. He wrote to his family and friend Pat about how much he missed home, how glad he would be when his year was up. On April 9th, yet another opportunity of sorts arose for him to leave Nui Loc: his mother was in a bad car wreck, and Tommy, desperate to hear her voice or at least get reassurance from home, requested to be allowed an emergency phone call home. His request was denied. His captain advised that the trip to Da Nang and the paperwork it involved would be too much trouble. Once again, Tommy stayed put. He was moved from slackman (second man) to pointman (first man) during the patrols.

Left: Tommy J. with an unidentified South Vietnamese Soldier

April 4, 67

Dear family,
I hope all is well. The pictures turned out pretty good I thought. I am in the process of taking a roll of color film now. It should be pretty good. We got our new rifles, the M16 Black Monster. It is a mean weapon and I like it. It looks like a space-age weapon. The V.C. are scared of it we know.

I like the pictures you sent also. It made me feel good to see you and Daddy looking real happy. That's what helps me a lot. Daddy looks real good.

What makes me feel so bad is knowing I can't help Daddy build the cabin. It could be enjoyed so much more if I had a hand in it. I feel like going out and telling VietNam where to go!

Photo sent to Tommy J. of his parents, Leila and T.J.

You know the feeling you get when it was morning at the mountains, and we would go jump in the river. A great feeling and I miss it so much. I guess that is what it would be like at the new lot.

We had a jet go down close to our mountain and we had to search for it. We had a lot of action before we found it and when we found it, it was a mess. The pieces were everywhere and only small pieces. No trace of the pilot at all. It was a sad mess. We were all hoping for the V.C. to hit us on the way back.

Well I had better close and get this letter off. Be good and don't worry.

Your son,

Tommy J.

April 4, 1967

Hi Pat,

How in the hell are you doing? I hope all is O.K. you 2/3's of a year college man.

We got our new weapons a few days ago and it is a mean, bad weapon. It even scares me. The Black Monster. I want to hurry and try it out on a damn V.C. He can hang it up. I sound bad, don't I?

Boy the nights here are even getting too hot to sleep. The bugs feast on you at night; it is getting just almost unbearable.

We had to search for a downed jet, just a little ways from our mountain, a few days ago. About 2/3's of the company went out and a lot of action was stirred up. When we finally found the plane, it was in all kind of pieces. The biggest piece could be picked up by hand. Not one trace of the pilot. I was so pissed off I was just hoping for the Charlie's to hit.

Last night a small hill just a little ways from us, which is manned by South Vietnamese and a few marines, was hit heavy. All kind of incoming rounds from all over.

We went on stand-by and thought we were going out. I am sure glad we didn't because it was too dark for me. We will reinforce it tonight. "Let them come!"

Well I guess I had better close for now and do something constructive. Like sit on my ass! Ha. Be bad!

Your ole pal,

Tommy J.

P.S. Why don't you send me some American pussy!

April 4, 67

Mr. & Mrs. Hogan,
I am really behind on letter writing, but we haven't had much free time lately. When you do get a little time, you have to take advantage of it and try to get some sleep. This is early morning, so maybe I will get to finish a letter.

We received our new rifles a couple of days ago and I sure like it. It is a real mean weapon and the V.C. are very scared of it. They call it a "Black Monster." I am just glad we have it and the V.C. doesn't. A jet airplane crashed just a little ways from our mountain the other day, while making a bombing mission. We sent almost our whole company, except for some security back at the mountain, to look for it. We ran into all kind of action getting there, and when we got there, the biggest piece of the plane could be picked up by hand. No trace at all of the pilot could be found. It was a bad site and it really made me mad. I was hoping for the V.C. to hit us on the way back.

I am glad Austin is fixing to rotate, and I know he is feeling good about now. One of these days I am going to get to Danang maybe and then I'll look up Ricky. You said he was at Red Beach I think. It would sure help to see somebody from Atlanta.*

Well I guess I will have to close and get this letter off.

Thanks for the letters and prayers. I will write more later.

Your friend,

Tommy Holtzclaw

---

* In 1963, Red Beach, in Danang Bay, the first American Marines had landed in Vietnam.

April 7, 67

Dear Daddy, Mother, and Johnny,
I just now received Johnny's letter telling me about Mother's accident. I almost fainted at first because it scared me so much. I tried to let the Captain let me make an emergency phone call home, but no luck. I would have to go to Danang, get permission from higher officers and other junk so he said just write home today and get all the information on her condition. If it was necessary for me to maybe call home, he would try to get me through. I can just see the pain she is going to have and all the trouble everyone will have around the house now. It really worries me. Everyone has got to pitch in and help now and don't expect Mother to work any for as long as the doctor says. All the money that comes in from me now will be used to help in any way it is needed. Don't hesitate to use it to buy anything or maybe pay those high doctors* [bills]. *I have enclosed a letter for Johnny to take to the bank giving him the right to withdraw any of my banking account when needed. Don't feel bad about using it, because I feel now like I maybe am doing you all some good.*

If anything else is needed let me know. Forget about sending those records for awhile and just get Mother well!

Johnny said he was the only one to be writing the letters for awhile, but I know Daddy can still push a pencil. It won't hurt him to write a sentence or two every once in awhile. Just to let me know how he is and still let me know he is remembering me.

If I know Kaye and Mrs. Bowman, they will pitch in, without you being able to stop them, to help anyway they can. Let everything go smooth and let me know what is going on. I love you all.

Will write more later.

Tommy J.

---

* The details of Mrs. Holtzclaw's car accident aren't fully known. The car flipped several times and she was in a coma. Her hair turned white from the shock.

April 10, 1967

Hello Mr. & Mrs. Hogan and family,
I received a letter and a box from you yesterday.

Thanks so much for remembering my birthday.

We had some real sad and disappointing action yesterday. We were on a patrol and had set in on an ambush. Around daylight, we sprung our ambush on a group of V.C. coming by. We got 7 of them but the rest got away. They then started firing back and we had a big firefight. We called in our artillery for support and it was hitting right on target. We then rushed their position to overrun it, and just before we got there, they opened up again. We got one of our men killed and 5 wounded. I have never had so many rounds hitting around me. I have not calmed down yet, I was so scared. We just had them trapped and they were fighting back. It was the first time I had got that close to a V.C. where I used my rifle to hit a V.C. There you really know how close you are to death. It is there also that you know you have actually had to kill and it is not a very good feeling.

Maybe I shouldn't have told you about this experience.

You wanted to know about our recreation. Till we came on the mountain, they would show movies and sell cokes. But here we don't have the facilities for it. We get papers in the mail and some of the guys have bought record players, so that is a little entertainment. But with all the operations, I don't have much time to get bored.

Sure glad to hear Mike will get to come home for a week-end. Only a short while and he and I will have one year of the service over. I'll be glad!

Some of the guys wanted to know if you were relatives because I get letters from you frequently. I tell them you are just my 2nd parents! Well I guess I will close now. I'll write more later.

Your friend,

Tommy

April 13, 1967

Pat,
I have been receiving your letters O.K. and it really helps to get them. It is awful hard to just leave all of your friends for over a year. I am expecting things to be like it was before I left but I know I will be disappointed. People getting married, going to service or school, and just getting older. Really, I don't want to grow up but I guess I have to.
I received a letter from Jimmy Portwood and Dennis Hamilton a few days ago. It was good to hear from them. We will have to have a big reunion around Christmas.

We just came off a company sized operation today. We got 7 V.C. in a 4 hour period with weapons and supplies. Then air strikes came in to bomb the area. One jet came in awful low and dropped a heat bomb. It exploded too soon and caught his tail end. He lost control and crashed into a mountain and exploded. It was a bad site and now a couple of platoons have to go search the area.

I guess you heard about my mother breaking a shoulder bone. She seems to be in quite a bit of pain and she is going crazy because she can't write very good left-handed. I wish I could see her.

Seems like Kaye and I will have an anniversary the 16th – one year. Seems very short to me. I sure will be glad to see her again. I miss her more than anything. I know what you mean about not wanting to lose Patsy, because I am the same way about Kaye.

Sure glad to hear about Mike's promotion; he will go far in the Corps.

I should make it before next month is over. At least that is what my C.O. says. We will see.

Well I guess I'll close for now and take a ride around the block in my new GTO.

Your ole pal,

Tom

April 14

Dear family,
I hope this finds you all O.K. I am doing fine. It is about 8:30 at night now and I am sitting here eating some Eagle Brand Milk. It sure is good if my buddy will quit eating it all.

I haven't received the records yet, but we aren't getting much mail at all. Thanks for sending them, I am sure they will get here soon. If you send a package anytime soon, maybe you can put me some stationery in it. I don't need envelopes but I do need a writing tablet. They haven't brought us any supplies up lately.

We are having a little rain now, the first in over a month. Most of the rice paddies are beginning to dry up now and it makes it better on the feet. We have another company size operation coming up in about 2 days and I hope it is as successful as the last.*

You wanted to know what I wanted for my birthday, but there is nothing I need really. So don't try to send anything, just wait till next year.

Mr. & Mrs. Hogan have really been friends. They write about once a week and have sent a few packages. I got a Birthday package from them a few days ago. They write a couple of other boys they know over here.

Well I guess I will close for now and mail this letter.

Don't worry.

Tommy

April 20

Hello family,
Been about 4 days since I have been able to write because we were out on a South Vietnamese soldiers' hill for security. We just got back here today and we are going out on a company operation tonight. It will be

* The "company operation" Tommy J. refers to was Operation Union, a search and destroy mission in the Que Son Valley carried out by the First Marine Regiment, 2nd Battalion.

hairy, because I have to walk point, or first man. Maybe we will have some success, there is suppose to be at least a squad of V.C. where we are going. I hope everything is O.K. and mother's arm is getting better. I received all the records and they sure bring pleasure to everyone.

Thanks so much for them.

I also got the birthday card, and I appreciate it. I am still considering myself 18 for 4 more days. I don't want to get older really.

I sure am sorry to hear "Dollar" [Carey "Dolla" Barber, Tommy's high school buddy] *wanting to come in the Marines. I wish I could talk to him and make him join the reserve or Navy or something easy. But if he wants action the Marine Corps is the one.* [Barber joined the Marines in 1967.]

Well I will close now and try to get a little sleep. Be good and I'll write more later.

Tommy

April 20

Here is a roll of color film I have made. When you take it to have it developed, tell them you want color pictures because it is really slide film. But they will make pictures. I hope they turn out O.K. because I got some good shots. Use my money.

Tommy

Last letter from Tommy J., undated

This is one pre-paid mailer with a roll of film in it that a buddy of mine made for me. All you have to do is take it to the same place as the other roll you will have developed and it will be developed free for you. The roll in the envelope you will have to pay for. I hope you understand. Thanks and I hope it won't be any trouble.

Tommy

Those may be slides also, tell them you want all color pictures not slides.

In mid-April of 1967, the commander of Tommy's company, Captain Gene A. Deegan, had advised the commander of the 1st Marine Regiment, Colonel Emil Radics, that enemy units appeared to be preparing for an all-out assault on the outpost of Nui Loc Son where Foxtrot was stationed. Deegan estimated the size of the enemy force to be at least two regiments in size. Accordingly, Radics developed a plan for a multi-battalion attack and sweep aimed at clearing NVA units from the vicinity of the mountain.

On April 20, Major General Herman Nickerson, the commanding general of the 1st Marine Division, approved the plan as "Operation Union," and it was put into action the following morning. What began as a routine sweep, however, turned into a 20-hour nightmare.

Acting as bait, Foxtrot Company was ordered to leave the mountain and to move down toward the nearest enemy-held village. On the morning of April 21, most of the Company set out on a daylight patrol that took them into the enemy-held village of Binh Son, in Quang Ngai Province. The 70,000 residents of Binh Son, formerly a French rubber plantation, had a long history of oppression by the French and Japanese, and were sympathetic to the Viet Cong and NVA.

Shortly after 7 a.m., as the Marines approached the village through the rice paddies, they were ambushed by a well-entrenched main force NVA battalion who benefited from a clear line of fire across level land with little cover. The first platoon, with Tommy J. as its pointman, was within 65 feet of the enemy trench line when they were suddenly struck by an avalanche of weaponry: hand grenades, rocket fire, rifle and automatic weapons and mortars. The Marines initially pushed the enemy back, but as the NVA center withdrew, their flanks moved forward to catch the advancing Marines in a "V" shaped trap.*

The onslaught killed 14 Marines and wounded 18, pinning the remainder of the platoon down in the rice paddies. Tommy J. was likely killed within minutes of the initial ambush. The remaining Marines tried to take cover behind the low paddy dikes, which the enemy then proceeded to blow away. The NVA had such well-prepared holes that artillery and air strikes had little effect. Unable to pull back, the Marines fought their way forward to the enemy-held treeline, where they stayed until darkness fell.

Source of battle description:

* http://www.geocities.com/operationunion/histories.html#hilgartner, see "April 21, 1967, *Sea Tiger* Article"

The fighting went on until well into the morning. Eyewitness accounts suggest that "most of the company" were either killed or wounded before they ever fought their way to Bin Son. "The fighting was so heavy and intense that it was four days before any wounded could be brought out," one source recalled**. One of the members of Mike Company, 3rd bn Fifth Marines, brought in to help the beleaguered Fox Company, recalled that Mike Company found "Fox Company [about 75 men]...on line half way across a rice paddy, most of them KIA."***

Accounts of this battle differ, one of them† claiming that at 11 am, Deegan moved his 2nd and 3rd platoons against the village of Bin Son, while the 1st platoon provided covering fire. Upon entering the village, all three platoons came under such heavy fire that, despite support from the 3rd bn First Marines, F Company was stuck and unable to maneuver their way out. The main body of the 3rd Battalion fought into the village to join Foxtrot in engaging the enemy while at approximately four p.m., the 3rd bn, 5th Marines arrived from Chu Lai east of the battle field, blocking the enemy's escape route and moving to link up with 3/1.

During the late afternoon, U.S. Army 175 mm self-propelled artillery and Marine 105 mm howitzers established separate firebases near the battlefield, and that evening, the 1st Battalion of the 1st Marine Regiment from Da Nang landed atop Nui Loc Son. By the next morning, the NVA had withdrawn from Binh Son and been driven northward. From that time until the end of Operation Union in mid-May, the enemy was hotly pursued by the U.S. Marines and the 1st ARVN Ranger Group in a series of battles that were costly to both sides: the NVA lost 865 troops, including a reported 486 NVA regulars of the 2nd NVA Division. The Marines suffered 110 KIA, 2 MIA and 473 wounded.

On May 26, 1967, Colonel Kenneth Houghton's 5th U.S. Marine Regiment, which had assumed control of the latter stages of Operation Union, kicked off Operation Union II. It is believed that Operation Union, together with the succeeding Operation Union II, inflicted over three thousand casualties on the PAVN.

Source of battle descriptions:

** http://www.voy.com/106095/ 128.html, photo caption

*** http://www.securenet.net/3rdbn5th/mike35/operations.htm, see B. 1967, Denny Dinota.

† http://1stbattalion 3rdmarines.com/operations-history-folder/union.htm

B52s Pound Major Route In Buffer Zone

SAIGON, April 23 (AP) — U.S. B52s carried out five raids against suspected Communist positions, including a bombing run on an infiltration route in the demilitarized zone between North and South Vietnam, the American command announced Sunday.

An Air Force B57 twin-engine Canberra light bomber was shot down by Viet Cong gunners 16 miles southeast of Saigon Saturday. The pilot was killed, but the navigator was rescued.

Over North Vietnam, U.S. pilots reported a brief encounter with Communist MIG17s Saturday. The MIGs broke contact as soon as the Air Force F105 Thunderchiefs positioned for attack, a spokesman said.

The American warplanes pounded North Vietnamese barracks, storage areas, boxcars and barges.

In ground action, only light contact was reported between U.S. Marines and Communist forces who earlier had fought a 20-hour battle 17 miles northwest of Tam Ky. The major fighting ended early Saturday.

The Marines revised upward the number of Communists killed in the two days of fighting from 46 to 96.

A Marine communique Saturday said a preliminary count showed 29 Marines killed and 94 wounded. But first reports by commanders in the field estimated that 60 Marines were killed and more than 100 wounded.

The Leathernecks clashed with the powerful Communist

B52s RAID

Continued from Page 1

force in a valley of coastal Quang Tin province, 375 miles northeast of Saigon.

For the second time in three days Saturday night, the eight-engined B52 Stratoforts struck at a major infiltration route, bivouac area and supply base in the demilitarized zones, 18 miles west of the South China Sea in Quang Tri province.

It is estimated that there are about 35,000 North Vietnamese troops in and around the zone.

IN PREDAWN raids Sunday, the B52s struck twice in Binh Duong province and twice in Tay Ninh province at suspected Communist base camps and supply areas.

In the two-day fight in Quang Tin province, nine U.S. helicopters were hit and two were downed during a battle that involved three Marine battalions.

With the flow of reinforcements, more than 1,500 Marines were committed to the battle before Saturday's dawn.

The action was stirred up Friday by a routine search and destroy mission of Foxtrot Company, 3rd Marine Regiment, near Tam Ky, an old tea and cinnamon trade center near the South China Sea.

It is in the lower section of the northern 1st Corps area, where American Marines have long formed the principal allied barrier.

The U.S. command disclosed it has set up a new Army task force, called Oregon, in that area. This means further fighting men will be available for field duty.

An article dated April 23, 1967 about Operation Union that appeared in the *Atlanta Journal Constitution*

Other Marines from Tommy J.'s Regiment who died on April 21, 1967

2nd Lt James H. Shelton, Hominy, Oklahoma

GySgt Roger D. Hamilton, Baltimore, Maryland

Sgt Edward D. Gould, Batesville, Arizona

Sgt Thomas A. Arredondo, Fresno, California

Cpl Gary R. Hartman, Newport, New York

Cpl James J. Owens, Woodside, New York

LCpl Vincent J. Benegas, Riverside, California

LCpl Byron D. Bonds, Evansville, Indiana

LCpl Rodney A. Breedlove, Alkol, West Virginia

LCpl James E. Carey, Altoona, Pennsylvania

LCpl John L. Davis, Conemaugh, Pennsylvania

LCpl Gary D. Grimes, Houston, Texas

LCpl Lanny R. Krage, Columbia, South Dakota

LCpl Larry C. Pettaway, Dayton, Ohio

LCpl Uvaldo Sanchez, Albuquerque, New Mexico

LCpl Ralph E. Scheib, Rochester, New York

Pfc Ronald M. Boley, New Lexington, Ohio

Pfc Benjamin Bunn, Washington, DC

Pfc Ronald R. Cormier, Portsmouth, New Hampshire

Pfc Edward T. Egan, Roslindale, Massachusetts

Pfc Sammy G. Evans, Hampton, Arizona

Pfc William D. Hunt, Birmingham, Alabama

Pfc Gary W. Martini, Portland, Oregon (Medal of Honor)

Pfc Maurice J. O Callaghan, Iselin, New Jersey

Pfc Eugene A. Pastrovich, C Walshville, Illinois

Pfc Dennis W. Pawlowicz, Duluth, Minnesota

Pfc Christopher Podmaniczky, St Louis, Missouri

CLASS OF SERVICE

This is a fast message unless its deferred character is indicated by the proper symbol.

WESTERN UNION TELEGRAM

W. P. MARSHALL, CHAIRMAN OF THE BOARD

R. W. McFALL, PRESIDENT

SYMBOLS

DL = Day Letter

NL = Night Letter

LT = International Letter Telegram

The filing time shown in the date line on domestic telegrams is LOCAL TIME at point of origin. Time of receipt is LOCAL TIME at point of destination

721P EST APR 23 67 AA305 PA461

P WA339 XV GOVT PD WASHINGTON DC 23 645P EST

MR AND MRS THOMAS J HOLTZCLAW JR, REPORT DELIVERY

1964 SUMTER ST ATLA

I DEEPLY REGRET TO CONFIRM THAT YOUR SON PRIVATE FIRST CLASS THOMAS J HOLTZCLAW III USMC DIED 21 APRIL 1967 IN THE VICINITY OF DANANG REPUBLIC OF VIETNAM. HE SUSTAINED A GUNSHOT WOUND TO THE BODY AS THE RESULT OF HOSTILE RIFLE FIRE WHILE ENGAGED IN ACTION AGAINST HOSTILE FORCES.

HIS REMAINS WILL BE PREPARED, ENCASED, AND SHIPPED AT NO EXPENSE TO YOU, ACCOMPANIED BY AN ESCORT, EITHER TO A FUNERAL HOME OR TO A NATIONAL CEMETERY SELECTED BY YOU. IN ADDITION YOU WILL BE REIMBURSED AN AMOUNT NOT TO EXCEED THREE HUNDRED DOLLARS TOWARD FUNERAL AND INTERMENT EXPENSES IF INTERMENT IS IN A PRIVATE CEMETERY, ONE HUNDRED FIFTY DOLLARS IF REMAINS ARE CONSIGNED TO A FUNERAL HOME PRIOR TO INTERMENT IN A NATIONAL CEMETERY, OR SEVENTY-FIVE DOLLARS IF REMAINS ARE CONSIGNED DIRECTLY TO A NATIONAL CEMETERY. PLEASE WIRE COLLECT HEADQUARTERS MARINE CORPS YOUR DESIRES IN THIS RESPECT, INDICATING THE NAME AND ADDRESS OF THE FUNERAL HOME OR NATIONAL CEMETERY TO WHICH YOU WISH THE REMAINS SENT AND WHETHER OR NOT YOU DESIRE AN ESCORT. THE MARIETTA NATIONAL CEMETERY, MARIETTA, GEORGIA IS NEAREST YOUR HOME. LETTER WILL FOLLOW CONCERNING CIRCUMSTANCES OF DEATH. I WISH TO ASSURE YOU OF EVERY POSSIBLE ASSISTANCE AND TO EXTEND THE HEARTFELT CONDOLENCES OF THE MARINE CORPS IN YOUR BEREAVEMENT

WALLACE M GREENE JR GENERAL USMC COMMANDANT OF THE MARINE CORPS.

SF1201(R2-65)

COMPANY F
1st Marines (Rein)
1st Marine Division (Rein), FMF
FPO, San Francisco, 96602

28 April 1967

Mr. and Mrs. Thomas J. Holtzclaw Jr.
1964 Sumter St.
Atlanta, Georgia

My dear Mr. and Mrs. Holtzclaw:

The recent death of your son Private First Class Thomas J. Holtzclaw III, U. S. Marine Corps, near Nui Lac Son, Quang Tin Province, Republic of Vietnam, is a source of sorrow to me and to his many friends in this company.

Thomas was a rifleman in our second platoon. On April 21, 1967 his platoon along with the other platoons from the company were on a company size operation when they came under fire from an estimated battalion of Viet Cong. During the ensuing fire fight Thomas was hit by one of the many bullets. There was a medical corpsman available, but there was nothing he could do to help. Thomas died instantly from the wound. There were a number of other casualties from the company and it is impossible to determine how many enemy casualties.

Thomas' quiet manner, eagerness to help and devotion to duty won him the respect of all who knew him. We in the company hope the knowledge that your son is keenly missed and that we share your sorrow will in some measure alleviate the suffering caused you by your great loss.

Thomas' personal effects have been prepared for shipment and will be forwarded to you shortly.

If you feel that I can be of any assistance, please do not hesitate to write.

Sincerely yours,

Edward J. Banks

EDWARD J. BANKS
Captain, U. S. Marine Corps
Commanding

O'Keefe Star War Victim

The tragedy of war came home starkly to O'Keefe High School and Coach Dan Kennerly Monday when it was learned that Tommy Holtzclaw, a "mighty mite" of the last three Irish football and soccer teams, was killed in action in Vietnam Friday.

"This news makes today one of the saddest of my 16 years of coaching here, because Tommy was undoubtedly one of the very finest youngsters I ever had," said Kennerly.

"Tommy was a 125-pounder with the heart of a 250-pounder, a reserve halfback in football and first string wigback two years in soccer. He was a solid A and B student and the kind who never missed a practice or an assignment in football and soccer.

"The telegram says he was killed in Danang Province by rifle fire. It seems like only yesterday he was a scrubby, likeable little eighth-grader. He was graduated last June and joined the Marines. Today would be his 19th birthday."

—ROBERTS

VICTIM

Thomas J. Holtzclaw Jr., of Atlanta, Ga., grandson of Mr. and Mrs. A. B. Davis of Iva, was killed in action in Vietnam April 21. Funeral services will be held Sunday at the Merina Baptist Church, Sumpter St., Atlanta, of which he was an active member. His parents, Mr. and Mrs. Thomas J. Holtzclaw reside in Atlanta.

The obituary that appeared in the *Atlanta Journal Constitution*

Office of the Governor
Atlanta

LESTER MADDOX
GOVERNOR

April 25, 1967

Dear friend Holtzclaw:

The sad news of your son's death reached me this morning. I know you have suffered a great loss, and no expression of sympathy, however sincere, can lighten the grief that has come to you. But you must find a measure of consolation in the realization that your son gave his life for his country.

Life and death are beyond our control and we must accept things as they are -- bravely. While no one has ever bridged the gap between this world and the next, I do believe that your son is still with you, and that he will keep right on being proud of the good things you do.

My prayers and thoughts are with you during your time of sorrow. May God bless you.

Sincerely,

Lester

Mr. Thomas J. Holtzclaw
1964 Sumter Street, N. W
Atlanta, Georgia

CA

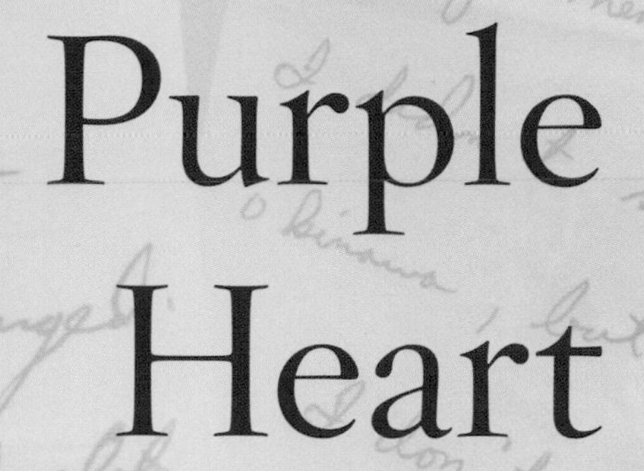

Purple Heart

CHAPTER EIGHT

In Atlanta, the Holtzclaws were in a state of shock. Tommy's letters were still arriving daily, along with official letters from the military telling of his death. Pictures he had taken, recently developed, showed him grinning and clowning with his buddies on the mountain, pointing at captured VC weapons, sitting in the sandbag bunkers with his unit, laughing as their picture was taken. Virginia Hogan remembered how agonizing it was for Tommy's parents, his sister and brother, as they awaited the return of his body from Vietnam. She and her husband went every night to sit with the Holtzclaws.

"Our hearts broke for them during the ordeal of Tommy's death," Virginia recalled, "and waiting so long for the body to arrive. We knew how hard this was on Mike and Pat and the other friends, as well as family. We could imagine ourselves in their position." She and her husband had one child in Vietnam; two more would soon follow. "Having met Skip and married in WWII, we never imagined another war and one that would involve our sons."

In accordance with Marine tradition, the Holtzclaws chose Mike Hogan, also by then in the Marines, to escort the body home, but Mike, in avionics school in Millington, Tennessee, had no idea that anything had gone wrong. He could not receive phone calls during the day, "so messages were taken at H.Q. and sent down to the barracks periodically." When the message came that said for him to call home immediately, Mike's first thought was that his parents were sick or had gotten hurt. Instead, his father answered the phone and told him that Tommy J. had been killed in action.

The last time Mike had seen Tommy was in the mess hall at Parris Island in 1966, when they were both in training and unable to talk to each other. Now, Tommy's father was requesting that Mike escort the body home. "I cried my guts out in that phone booth," Mike said, "then went back to the barracks. Later I was called up to H.Q. to get instructions on escort duty. I borrowed some dress blues from a friend and was sent to the Philadelphia naval yard for escort training. We went to Dover, Del[aware] air force base to pick up Tommy's body. There were three continuous buildings about three football fields long with tables. There were bodies on almost all those tables. Those were the ones they were working on, but a lot were like Tommy, classified as unviewable remains. So they put those bodies in caskets, covered all but the head with sheets, and put a set of dress blues on top of the sheets."

Mike flew home with Tommy's body to Atlanta, where his remains were moved to the Frank B. Lowndes & Son funeral home on 14th Street, in preparation for the service at Marantha Baptist Church on May 4. Mr. Holtzclaw and Tommy's younger brother Johnny accompanied Mike to the funeral parlor. It's hard to imagine how difficult this would have been for them all; Tommy had been killed on the 21st of April; by now, it was the first of May, two weeks later.

"We were taught to discourage the family from looking at the remains, but I didn't stress that with Tommy's dad, only his mom," Mike recalled, "as I know how easy mistakes can be made, and if it was my son

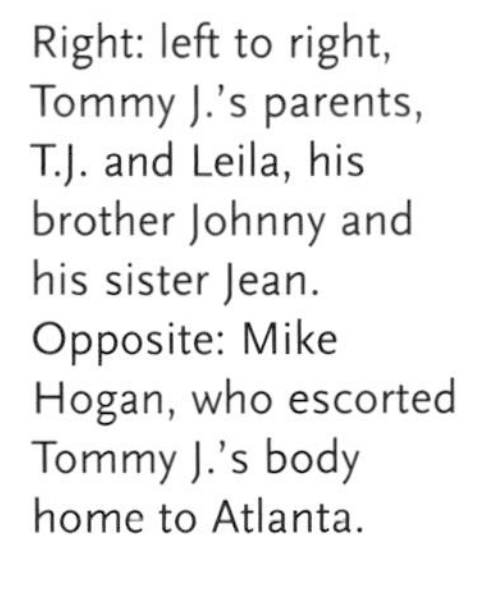

Right: left to right, Tommy J.'s parents, T.J. and Leila, his brother Johnny and his sister Jean. Opposite: Mike Hogan, who escorted Tommy J.'s body home to Atlanta.

CORPS

Tommy J.'s sister Jean and her husband J.C. at the funeral home. On May 4, 1967 Tommy J.'s body was interred at Crest Lawn Cemetery in Atlanta, Georgia; Section 36, Lot 343, Space 1

I would want to know for sure in my own mind. So T.J. Sr., Johnny [Holtzclaw] and I went into the funeral home backroom and viewed the body. We could tell it was him by his distinctive profile, as his head was turned to the side."

In the days and weeks following Tommy's funeral, his sister Jean's emotional stability collapsed; her two children were sent to live with their father's parents for six months. T.J. and Leila blamed each other for signing Tommy's enlistment application. Terri Campbell Walker says no one really talked about their feelings after the loss of Tommy J. Her grandmother Leila explained the terrible anguish she and T.J. Senior felt in one brief remark: "It's hard to comfort the other when you can't comfort yourself." She told Terri that losing Tommy had almost torn them apart.

Johnny Holtzclaw started driving his brother's car, but ultimately had to sell it. Every time he passed the cemetery (en route to the Holtzclaws' residence at 1964 Sumter Street), the interior light would start blinking. Everything connected to Tommy was too painful for the family to deal with, even sharing their memories of him. As time wore on, an unspoken rule developed: No one was to talk about Tommy J. The silence was better than remembering the loss.

May 24, 1967

Dear Mr + Mrs Campbell,

Thank you so much for all the expressions of Sympathy during our time of sorrow. your Card, letter and flowers were most appreciated.

Most of all, thanks for keeping Connie and Terri for Jean and J.C. Bless their hearts, they were too little to understand our unhappiness.

Part of us died when our Tommy was killed. There will always be something missing. We know that he is in heaven waiting for us to come to him. It seemed that he was saying "Look up here, mother - I'm up here." I thank God for that.

I know you were here with us in prayers and thoughts. Just wish you could have been here in person. I know you did the most needed thing at the time. Connie and Terri needed to be away from all the sorrow and you gave your 100 per cent.

I hope you are both well and happy. We are doing as well as we can.

Come to see us when you Can. Love -

Leila - T.J. - Johnny Holtzclaw

A letter from Tommy J.'s mother, Leila to Charlie and Leola Campbell, who were J.C's parents. Jean broke down at the news of her brother's death, and her husband's parents stepped in to care for the children.

His niece Terri remembers being curious about her uncle and how the topic was simultaneously appealing and off limits. "There was a victrola in the corner of our formal living room," she recalled. It had always been part of the décor, covered with a piece of purple velvet, with Tommy's high school pictures and his formal Marine portrait set on top, along with pictures of the funeral. But no one would tell her anything except that he had been killed in Vietnam. "Any time I asked questions, it just created sadness, and I eventually just stopped asking."

When Leila Holtzclaw died in September of 2006, Terri found in a box of mementoes a copy of the 1966 O'Keefe graduation program and looked for names that were linked with Tommy's. She found Jimmy Portwood on an internet search site and called him. Jimmy had recently been to an O'Keefe reunion and was able to contact Mike Hogan. Mike called about a week later, and Carey "Dolla" Barber called her out of the blue. These friends of Tommy's, and other members of the Hogan family, began to help Terri put the puzzle pieces of her uncle's short life into place.

Connie Campbell Hughes with her two children, Dustin (Dusty) Keith Peters and Tabitha Jean Peters.

Though she was older than Terri when their uncle died, Terri's sister Connie Campbell Hughes barely recalls Tommy J. She still has a stuffed animal he gave her, "a big red stuffed dog... It is missing an eye, an ear, its fur is almost completely gone but I cannot bring myself to get rid of it." Connie feels that she got to know Tommy J. mostly by reading his letters from Vietnam. Two years ago when she went to Parris Island, where her uncle trained to become a Marine, all she was able to think about was "how he must have felt being there, what he went through and the man he became."

For Pat Hogan, who knew Tommy better, perhaps, than anyone else, the letters are all he has of a friendship that once meant the world to him—a "running buddy," a best friend, and a boy unafraid to write what he really thought, whether it meant expressing his hopes about Pat's future or his own doubts about the war he was fighting.

It has been said of many Vietnam veterans, that although they made it home, they left their souls in Vietnam. Tommy J.'s soul remains intact in these letters. More than just a chronicle of his days in Vietnam, the letters reveal his fears and joys and worries, the day-to-day activities and the business of war. In the course of producing this collection, the people he left behind have been able to finally express emotions once too difficult to even talk about. They have been able to share their memories of the dark days when Tommy J. lost his life, to talk, once again, about this boy everyone loved so dearly. The letters have formed a bridge from the past to the present.

In many ways, it is as if Tommy has finally come back home.

"My Nephew: A United States Marine"

My nephew was a boy, who was always cheerful and gay.
Who was always laughing, joking, and smiling each day.
He was loved and respected by everyone at the school he attended
And in all things that came up for a vote, He was recommended.
He was on the football squad, and did he make them scream
Until they finally elected him Capt. of the team.
He was a natural born leader in everything he undertook.
When others would get stranded he would get them off the hook.
And when he had finished High School and left it behind
There was one thing more he wanted to get off his mind.
And that was his military obligations, for you see,
Until it was over he could never be free.
So he signed up for service with the U.S. Marines
And after boot training, He served in places he had never seen.
First to California for a few lessons and briefs
And then he was packed up and sent overseas.
All of this was very exciting and something new to him.
But soon he found out he was being sent to South Vietnam.
Although this was discouraging he did not complain.
For he knew that "God" was with him and "God" would reign.

But as the days passed on and turned into weeks,
He ran into things he said would give him the creeps.
So much of this killing and hunger and strife.
He had never seen anything like this in all of his life.
As he fought each day and night through thick and thin,
His one thought was what he could do when it came to an end.
He would send his pay home each time he was paid

And tell Mom, take "God's" out first and the rest is to be saved.
For he was planning on being married when he came home.
And just settle down, he and his wife, in a home of their own.
He had lots and lots of things planned to do.
That is the reason he wanted to get his military duty through.
The letters he wrote home were never complaining or blue,
He would always have something else in mind to do,
Such as write of the more beautiful things he had seen,
Like the beautiful rivers and mountain tops so high and green.
He always seemed so cheerful and gay in his letters to you.
That I finally got where I could relax for a moment or two.
Until one day in 1967, the Marine Chaplain gave us a call.
We knew something had happened, I could almost feel myself fall.
The Marine Capt. tried to tell us what had happened to our son
And said a telegram would follow telling how it was done.
The telegram then came after so long a time.
And after it was read I almost lost my mind.
It said he died in action fighting for the Country he loved
And now I know that he has gone on to "Heaven above."
"God" does things sometimes in mysterious ways.
Ways that many of us can't understand at all
But we should always be ready, When "God" gives the call.
One thing I am proud of and cherish and love,
Is the testimony he left after he had gone on above.
Everyone who ever knew him and even those he had not seen,
Mourned and grieved at the death of this wonderful nephew of mine
A United States Marine.

Dedicated to one I will always love and cherish:
My Nephew Tommy J. Holtzclaw

— James D. Steading

To Tommy — Our Friend

Heaven was even crying,
When Tommy was laid to rest.
I know God's heart was breaking;
He loves the small bird in the nest.
How could He fail to see,
The tears in our eyes and my heart,
As we watched the earthly body,
Of our dear friend depart.
In our memories, Tommy will always
Be one of the "Gallant Men."
We're so grateful we could know him,
And that we could call him friend.
In this swift journey of life,
We stop and thank God for this boy,
Who brought in a few short years,
To others, so much love and joy.
There are those who will never know him
But how could we ever forget.
There will always be dark moments,
When we will doubt and regret,
That Tommy could not stay with us longer,
But we do not understand.
Our hearts have such narrow vision
To see the Creators plan.
Though we are troubled and weeping
Tommy's soul is at peace and rest.
When the time came to fulfill his purpose,

He quietly passed the test.
What greater legacy could he leave
In this world of turmoil and strife;
To us, who would achieve our purpose
Than the example of his love and his life.
Tomorrow Heaven will be smiling.
And, as I gaze on the green countryside.
I'll think of the beautiful look on his face
As in the bright sunlight, he died.

— Jean Hogan
May 4, 1967

Greater love hath no man, than that this man lay down his life for his friend.

— John 15:13

Tommy J.'s mother Leila and his niece, Terri C. Walker, point to his name on the Vietnam Veterans Memorial Wall. It is located on Panel 18E, Line 60.

Afterword

How tragic that someone who inspired such poetry and tributes was lost to us before he had the opportunity to make the impact in the world that was his true destiny.

I was born September 21, 1964, only three years before Tommy J. was killed on April 21, 1967. I never had the opportunity to know him. Those who did never fully recovered from losing this man who was willing to give his life for this great country.

The bravery he shows in his letters and the ability to show how scared he was makes me proud. But it also makes me cry. Many of the horrors he saw during his four months in Vietnam, he was never able to put into words. Despite his fears, and facing battle day and night, Tommy J. worried about his family and tried his best to participate in their lives, even insisting that they use his pay at home to buy clothing and gifts for themselves. He requested very little other than the occasional "care package" with the most basic necessities unavailable in Vietnam. Even though he was at war, he took the time to write home almost every day. He worried about his friends and family, and encouraged his closest friends and his brother to stay in school and not expose themselves to the dangers of war. All Tommy asked for himself was to stay in their hearts and prayers.

Every letter Tommy J. wrote tells me he was a loving man . . . a caring man . . . a gentleman.

— Terri C. Walker

About the Editor

Gina Webb is a writer and editor who has worked with a variety of publishers in Atlanta, including Turner Publishing, Longstreet Press and Lionheart Books. From 1995-1997, she was the music editor at *Creative Loafing,* Atlanta's alternative newspaper. Her work has appeared in such publications as the *Atlanta Journal-Constitution*, the *Chattahoochee Review* and *Southern Voice*. Following Hurricane Katrina's devastation of New Orleans, she wrote and co-edited the CNN-produced *Katrina, State of Emergency*. Originally from New Jersey, she has lived in Atlanta since 1978.

Acknowledgments

Without the cooperation of each individual involved in this project, a book like this would never have been possible. I would first like to thank Terri Walker, whose courageous decision to publish her uncle's letters—and to let me edit them—gave me the opportunity to get to know Tommy J. Holtzclaw, and, through him, to see the Vietnam War and those who gave their lives for it, from a different perspective. I would also like to thank the Hogans—Jean, Steve, Mike and especially Pat—and Jim Portwood, for so generously sharing their memories of Tommy J. With their help, I was able to develop a picture of him that I hope represents something of the person he was and could have been. I am also indebted to the person responsible for my inclusion on this project, Laurie Shock, whose unerring design sense, friendship and guidance were invaluable in all ways. I wish also to thank my companion Michael Holbrook for his advice and indispensable help with reconstructing Atlanta and Marietta, Georgia, of the 1950s-60s. Lastly, I would like to remember Joseph Dennis Roman, 1944-2006, who also served in Vietnam.

"It is awful hard to believe war."

— Thomas J. Holtzclaw, III